A Sketch
of
Hornsea

From Domesday Book to 1901

J.E. Hobson

Revised Edition
Edited by
Mike Sewell and Frank Hobson

First edition published in 1974 by the Author
Revised edition published in 2002 by Hornsea Museum

The North Holderness Museum of Village Life
11 Newbegin, Hornsea, East Yorkshire, HU18 1AB

CONTENTS

ACKNOWLEDGEMENTS 1974

In the writing of this book I have received help and encouragement from a great number of people and it gives me great pleasure to acknowledge all the many kindnesses I have received.

First of all I should like to thank Mr. David Neave, B.A., organising tutor of the W.E.A., both for his many helpful suggestions and for reading through parts of the manuscript. Thanks are due also to three members of the staff of Endsleigh College, Mr. G. Williams and Miss P. Atkinson for material and Mr. G. Flynn for Latin translations.

I would like also to acknowledge permission to use details from the Borthwick Institute publication "Medieval Clerical Accounts". The staff of the Hull Local History Library were always helpful during my many visits and the East Riding Archivist, Mr. Higson produced for my benefit every document relating to Hornsea and Hornsea Burton in the County archives.

Invaluable help with maps and copies of documents was given to me by Miss B.M. Shackles, Mr. M. Green, A.R.I.B.A. and Mr. K. Cline. The latter also gave much information about milling. The late Mr. Walter Robinson contributed his account of the Primitive Methodist Chapel.

Mrs. E. Harry and Mr. A. Hobson very kindly wrote down their recollections for me and Dr. H.I. Loten allowed me to use his father's account of town life and his own schoolday memories. Thanks are also due to Mrs. A. Hobson, Miss Garbutt, Mr. C. Burton, Mrs. A. Brumby (then 102 years old!) and Mr. F. Train for much useful information which they so generously gave and also to Mr. M. Lonsdale.

I am also greatly indebted to Mrs. J. Hines, now living in Oregon, U.S.A., who typed nearly three quarters of the book, working steadily through the most complicated network of corrections, and also to Mrs. M. Lansdell, Mrs. B. Kilby, Mr. F. Hobson and Mrs. B. Leng who typed the remainder.

Finally I must thank my husband who not only corrected all the punctuation throughout the manuscript, but also lived with "The Book and I" for four long years.

ACKNOWLEDGEMENTS 2002

The Trustees of Hornsea Museum are very grateful to Jean Smith, (J.E. Hobson,) for her generosity in transferring the copyright of "A Sketch of Hornsea" to the Museum and also for allowing the publication of this revised edition, which has been undertaken in the light of more recent research into some aspects of Hornsea's history. The major part of the original text has withstood well the test of time in the nearly 30 years since the book was first published.

The cover picture shows St. Nicholas' church Hornsea as it looked around 1840 before the Victorian restoration. The engraving was originally published in George Poulson's "History of Holderness."

FOR MY FATHER

HORNSEA
The Origin of the Name

According the "The Place Names of the East Riding of Yorkshire and York," by A.H. Smith, 1937, the "-sea" part of the name comes from Old English, with the meaning of "pool" or "lake." This must refer to Hornsea Mere. "Horn" is also Old English and means "headland" or "projecting piece of land." Thus, the name Hornsea can probably be translated as, "lake in which lies a projecting piece of land." This probably refers to the peninsula of Kirkholme which lies at the eastern end of the Mere. "Kirkholme" comes from Old Scandinavian, and is usually translated as, "raised piece of ground in a marsh near a church."

PREFACE

Through the centuries the place now called "HORNSEA" has had many changes of fortune. The Saxon-Danish settlement called "HORNESSE" in the Domesday Book became in the 13th Century the prosperous market town "HORNSE" with its companion small port of "HORNSE BEK."

By the middle of the 15th Century "HORNSSE" could boast of two market days a week and together with "HORNSSE BEK" and "HORNSSE BURTON" had become the fifth most important settlement in the East Riding.

The destruction of "HORNSEYE BEK" in the 16th Century led to the decline in the fortunes of "HORNSEYE" so that by the middle of the 17th Century the town, now spelt "HORNSEY" in the Manor Court Rolls, had dwindled in size to be scarcely larger than a village and a poor one at that.

With the innovation of sea bathing in the 18th Century prosperity returned to "HORNSEY" and in the 19th Century with the building of the railway "HORNSEA" had regained all its former importance.

The following pages attempt to portray these changes in the history of the town beginning with the entry in Domesday Book and ending with the death of Queen Victoria.

The Parish of Hornsea in 1850

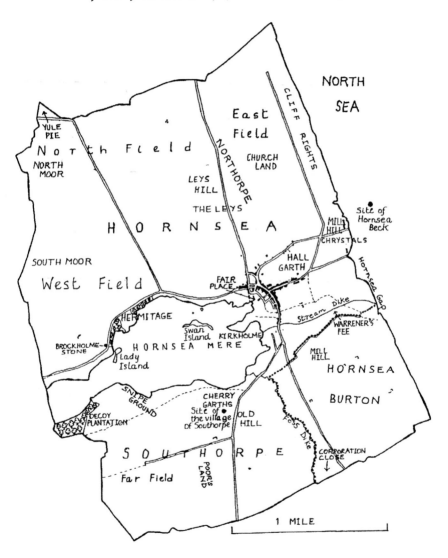

NORTH SEA

YULE PIE

NORTH MOOR

N o r t h F i e l d

East Field

NORTHORPE

CLIFF RIGHTS

CHURCH LAND

LEYS HILL

THE LEYS

H O R N S E A

Site of Hornsea Beck

MILL HILL

CHRYSTALS

SOUTH MOOR

West Field

HALL GARTH

FAIR PLACE

Hornsea Gap

HERMITAGE

Swan Island

KIRKHOLME

Stream Dike

WARRENER'S FEE

BROCKHOLME-STONE

Lady Island

HORNSEA MERE

MILL HILL

H O R N S E A

SNIPE GROUND

CHERRY GARTHS

Site of the village of Southorpe

OLD HILL

Foss Dyke

BURTON

DECOY PLANTATION

CORPORATION CLOSE

S O U T H O R P E

Far Field

POOR'S LAND

1 MILE

Hornsea in the Domesday Survey

In hornesse ht Morcar. xx vij. car.ad gld
7 road car poll ibi.ee. Ne ht Drogo ibi. i. car.
7 Wizo ho ei. i. car. 7 viji. uill 7 iij. bord. cu. i. car
7 dim. Ibi eccia 7 pbr. 7 lx. acf pa.

As hoc ai pinet t foca. Buraine. Torp. Rifruna
Schireflai. S dierelaine
Simul ad gld. xi. car tie. 7 dimid. ubi poll ee.
xii. car. Ne ht Drogo ibi. ii. loth 7 iiij. uill cu. ii car.
T.R.E. uat. lvi. lib. m xi lib.

The Hornsea Entry in Domesday Book, 1086

After the Norman Conquest in 1066 King William continued to levy the Danegeld, the payments used to bribe the Danes not to attack England. William used the money so raised to finance his government. To prepare an exact account of all the taxable property in the realm in continuance of this policy it was decided in the winter of 1085 to send commissioners to every shire of England to gather all the details of the wealth of the country.

The enquiries made by the King's men were very detailed, so much so that, as an English chronicler of the time indignantly observed, "So very narrowly he let speer it out that there was not a single hide nor a yard of land, nor so much as an ox nor a cow nor a swine was left that was not set in his writ." These details were gathered together in the Domesday Book, so called because it seemed no more possible to appeal from it than from the Last Judgment.

Part of the North had been cruelly devastated by William in 1070 in revenge for the rebellion of the Northern Earls in the preceding year. In this rebellion the Earls were joined by a Danish fleet which had raided inland as far as York and destroyed many of the Norman garrisons. In retribution the Vale of York was pillaged by William and large areas were still "waste land" at the time of the survey 15 years later. The East Riding had escaped most of the reprisals, and only a few villages along the Wolds suffered in this destruction. Holderness had only three villages out of 39 listed as being "waste". The survey shows a higher proportion of Norman names - Nigel, Richard, Hugh and Robert - for the Manors along the Wolds. Elsewhere in the Riding the Scandinavian names Torchil, Siward, Ulf, Grim, Ingrad, Carle, Elaf, Otre, Alden, Tochi, Edulf, Knut, Alric. - show how complete had been the takeover of the land by the invading Danes in the previous century.

At the time of Domesday the population of Holderness has been calculated as being between 2-5 people per square mile. These people, many of Danish origin, lived in the small settlements, founded originally by the Saxons, which have grown into the villages of today. Holderness was then the most prosperous part of the East Riding. Compared to the thin soil of the Wolds the thick boulder clay was fertile and could support the maximum number of plough teams. Because most of the drainage of the area was poor the settlements were on the higher, better drained land which stood out like islands from the surrounding marshland. Small fresh water lakes, or meres as they are known locally, abounded with a consequent number of fisheries which were recorded in the survey. The semi-marshland comprising most of the countryside could support only a thin cover of poor small trees; Holderness was always short of good timber and only at Beverley and on the south Wolds were entries made in the Domesday survey of sizeable woodlands.

The Domesday Book entry for Hornsea says,

In Hornesse Morcar had 27 carucates of land to be taxed and there may be as many ploughs there, Drogo has now there one plough and Wizo his vassal one plough and nine villeins and three bordars with one plough and a half. There is a church and priest and 60 acres of meadow.
To this manor belongs the soke of these. Burtune two carucates, Torp one carucate and a half, Ristune two carucates and six oxgangs, Schireslai six oxgangs, Skereltune five carucates altogether rated to the Danegeld at eleven carucates and a half where there may be twelve ploughs. Drogo has now there two sokemen and three villeins with two ploughs. Value in King Edwards time 56 pounds, now six pounds.

A carucate of land was the amount of land ploughed by one plough team, of eight oxen, in one year, and was usually estimated at 120 acres. An oxgang was the amount of land that one ox could plough in a year, usually estimated at 15 acres although both these measurements would obviously vary with the nature of the land. A soke was an area over which the lord of the manor had some rights; the right to hold a court for instance, but not complete ownership. Of the settlements mentioned as being in "the soke of Hornesse," Burtune (Hornsea Burton) had about 240 acres of ploughland and Torp (Southorpe) 180. The 3 plough teams accredited to Hornesse (Hornsea)

2

at the time of the survey, i.e. 1086 would presumably have ploughed about 420 acres. This would indicate the relative importance of the settlement of Hornsea which is confirmed by the building of the church there. This church would probably be a small wooden building with a thatched roof.

The Earl Morcar, Earl of Northumbria, the lord of "Hornesse" before the Conquest was a very powerful and wealthy man who had rebelled against William in 1069. After his defeat his lands were given by William to one of his followers, Drogo de la Beuvrière.

The part of the entry dealing with the pre-Conquest amount of ploughland and the number of plough teams in Hornsea - "27 carucates of land to be taxed and there may be as many ploughs there," (i.e. 27 ploughs,) is puzzling. Hornsea was one of five places entered on one page of Domesday, which were assessed at £56 tax paid before 1066, the five were in summary:

Brostewic	(Burstwick)	£56 now £10
Chilnesse	(Kilnsea)	£56 now £10
Witfornes	(Withernsea)	£56 now £6
Mappletone	(Mappleton)	£56 now £6
Hornesse	(Hornsea)	£56 now £6

In these manors there were very large variations between the number of plough teams and ploughland although the tax said to have been paid in 1066 was the same. However all these places were difficult to reach from any central point of the East Riding; the marshy nature of Holderness meant that many places became isolated during the late winter and early spring months, the time of year when the commissioners were gathering their information. One historian assumes from these figures that a certain area of land would have a given amount of "geld" to be distributed over it but later confesses, "As to the Yorkshire figures, we think that, of all the figures in Domesday, they are the least likely to be telling us the simple truth about the amount of cultivated land". There is one other factor which could be important in the high assessments of these five manors; they were all held directly by Drogo de la Beuvrière.

Drogo was a Flemish adventurer who had thrown in his lot with the Norman invaders in 1066. In return William awarded him some of the land held by Earl Morcar including the Lordship of Holderness. Drogo built a castle at Skipsea, traces of which still remain. He proved to be a cruel, grasping, ruthless man, prepared to go to any lengths to increase his power, even, according to a Domesday entry, by taking land from the Church. He had married a kinswoman of King William and in 1085 he murdered her. To escape the punishment he deserved he obtained leave from William to travel to Flanders before news of the murder reached the court thus escaping punishment since William had no jurisdiction in Flanders.

At the time of the gathering of the details for the Domesday

3

survey he was an outlaw and his lands were forfeit. Usually in the case of the death of an owner, details were left out of the survey. But in this case very high figures are entered for the outlaw's lands. A check through the details given for the rest of the villages in Holderness reveals that the plough teams elsewhere in Holderness owned by Drogo de la Beuvrière were assessed at double the figure set for his tenant plough teams or the other holders of land, e.g. the Church or the Norman landowners. Of the five manors owned by Drogo de la Beuvrière and assessed so highly for tax purposes two, Withernsea and Burstwick, were retained by the Crown after confiscation from Drogo, Burstwick being a favourite Royal hunting lodge up to the reign of Edward II.

The successor to Drogo de la Beuvrière as Lord of Holderness was a Norman, Odo, Count of Champagne who became Lord Seigniory of Holderness in 1086. It was Count Odo who gave the manor of Hornsea with the church, the Mere and the soke of Thorpe to the abbey of St. Mary's without the walls of York, in whose possession they remained until the dissolution of the monasteries.

When Odo rebelled against King William's son, William Rufus, his lands were forfeited and given to William le Gros, Count of Aumale. On several occasions over the next 300 years the Lordship of Holderness was claimed by the Crown. In the reign of Elizabeth I it was granted to Sir John Constable of Burton Constable whose descendant is still today entitled to claim to be Lord Seigniory of Holderness.

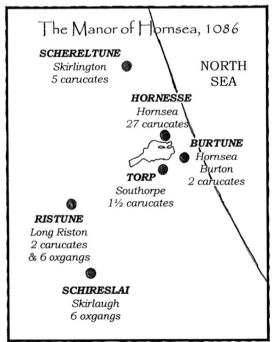

The Manor of Hornsea, 1086

SCHERELTUNE
Skirlington
5 carucates

NORTH
SEA

HORNESSE
Hornsea
27 carucates

BURTUNE
Hornsea
Burton
2 carucates

TORP
Southorpe
1½ carucates

RISTUNE
Long Riston
2 carucates
& 6 oxgangs

SCHIRESLAI
Skirlaugh
6 oxgangs

Hornsea was the principal settlement of the manor, which also had manorial jurisdiction over specified amounts of land in five other settlements. This dependent territory was known as a soke and was normally farmed by free tenants called sokemen. However, according to Domesday Book, the soke of Hornsea was farmed by two sokemen and three villeins, (who were unfree peasants.) Hornsea itself was farmed by Wizo who controlled nine villeins and three bordars, (who were smallholders.)

4

2 Hornsea under the Abbey of St. Mary's

For the next 450 years the Manor of Hornsea was owned and administered by the Abbey of St. Mary without the walls of York. There are few documents available to give any picture of Hornsea under the rule of the Abbey; those few details available are to be found in a series of disputes over the right to hunt and to fish in the Manor of Hornsea which the Abbey claimed as belonging to the lordship of the Manor.

Fishing disputes

Perhaps the most valuable part of the manorial rights was the right to fish in the Mere. In Medieval times the winter diet relied on salt meat and small quantities even of that; the fresh fish of the Mere would be a much sought after alternative. There were several disputes between St. Mary's and other landowners over the fishing rights. In January 1251 a William Lascelles, a tenant at Wassand, claimed that the right of fishing in the Mere had belonged to the tenant of his land since the reign of King John. The Abbot of Meaux Abbey, a forceful, acquisitive man, seems to have been behind this claim, for William Lascelles had agreed to surrender the right to fish to Meaux Abbey if he won. This dispute was brought before the Justices at York, (as were all the other disputes,) and, in the spirit of the age, a trial by combat was arranged. William, "... offered the body of Stephen of Barkedal his free man. The Abbot of St. Mary's in his turn offered the body of his free man, John Sutton". The combat took place on February 2nd and lasted all day and the Abbot's champion was adjudged the winner.

The unfortunate William Lascelles gave up his claim to the fisheries in return for 2 marks of the Abbot's rent in Holderness. The Abbot of St. Mary's, apparently in revenge, then attempted to dispossess William of his own land at Wassand, for in 1252 a complaint was heard by the Justices in which:-

> "The Abbot and Roger the sergeant are accused that they unjustly disseissed William de Lascelles of his free tenement in Wantsound (Wassand) and Burton and further claims they disseissed him of two marks of land and rents which the Abbot granted William by a fine at the last itinerary in the county in return for a certain fishpond (sic) touching which a duel was fought between them in the same court, the Bailiff of the Liberty of Holderness assigned him land of 2

marks and rent and by seissin he took 5
shillings rent and was in seissin until the
Abbot elected him."

Another dispute over the fishing rights took place in 1280; this
time a Robert de Ros claimed the right to have one boat on the Mere to
fish daily in an area defined as being:-

"... from the boundary between Hornse field
and Seton field and then across in a line to the
boundary between Wassand and Southorpe
field in the south side so East to the causeway
dividing Hornse Mere from Hornse Burton
Mere."

(During excavation some years ago at the end of what is now
called Bogeymar's Lane, a cobbled roadway was uncovered several feet
below the surface. This could well have been the "causeway" referred to
in this settlement.) The rent that Robert Ros was to pay for this privilege
was to be 6d at Martinmas and a pair of furred gloves; however the right
to fish was only his so long as he held Garton Manor.

A final dispute over the fishing was in 1439 and involved a John
Lorymer of Seaton, gentleman, Richard Towton of Seggistorn
(Sigglesthome) chapman and John Worrener of Gousell (Goxhill)
yeoman, who were accused of taking fish to the value of
£10 in the Abbot's several fisheries.

Hunting disputes

The Abbey was also entitled to hunt certain animals over the Manor
Lands. In 1232 the Abbot was a plaintiff in an action against the Count
of Aumale, (Lord Seigniory of Holderness,) in which the Abbot claimed
that the Count:-

"... did not permit the Abbot and his men of
Hornesse with their hare hounds to take hares
within the bounds of the Manor of Hornesse
which right the Abbot has by gift from the
Count's ancestor."

This right was claimed again by the Abbot in 1266 against the
men of Walter de Fauconberg, "... wherefore they entered the Abbot's
free warren at Hornesse and hunted and took away hares without the
Abbot's leave". The de Fauconbergs held 2 oxgangs of land in Hornsea
Burton from the Count of Aumale. The right to warren, (hunt hares and
rabbits,) in Hornsea and Hornsea Burton was also claimed by Meaux
Abbey and this right was confirmed by charter in 1327.

6

Farming

The manorial lands of Hornsea would have been tilled by the villeins who would have to work on the lord's land for so many days each year. In return they would have the right to work as tenants on their own strips of land, handing over each year a percentage of their produce to the Abbot's bailiff, who apparently supervised several manors. Mention is made of this bailiff in an action in 1344 between the Abbot and a Stephen de Apilton who was asked, "... to render an account of the time when he was Abbot's Bailiff and Receiver in Hornesse, Spaunton and Grymston."

In the average manor, the food for the community was produced from three very large open fields. However, in areas where the soil was poor, or difficult to cultivate, a two field system was used. This seems to have been the practice throughout the clay land of Holderness. Hornsea was no exception; the two large fields of Hornsea were called East Field and West Field; in the neighbouring hamlet of Southorpe the village fields were called Far Field and Hither Field.

To obtain an equitable share in the good soil available, the fields were divided into hundreds of strips and each villager held a selection of these strips. The crops grown were of two kinds, the winter sown crops such as wheat and rye sown between Michaelmas (September 29th) and Christmas and the spring sown crops of barley, vetches, oats, peas and beans. Both the winter and spring sown crops matured in August or September and both were harvested at the same time. To maintain the fertility of the soil, under the three field system, one of the three fields was left fallow each year. Under the two field system, as in Hornsea, one field was left fallow each alternate year.

The drainage of the land, very essential on the heavy boulder clay of Holderness, was helped by the system of ploughing. The plough would enter a strip of land at the left of centre and plough down the strip, then back up the outer edge of the strip; thus, as the mould board was on the right of the plough blade, the earth was heaped into a ridge; these ridges were a furrow long, which gave the name furlong. These wide long ridges can still be seen at Southorpe in the field west of the main road, at Hornsea Burton and along the Seaton Road. Obviously the soil at the top of the ridge would be drained by the water running down the ridge side into the depression between the neighbouring ridges and from there draining finally into a ditch.

It seems to have been usual for neighbours in the village to have adjoining strips in the fields; this would help in sharing the work and deciding the day's task. The teams which drew the plough were of oxen, eight yoked in pairs, the four yokes in line. Two men would follow the plough, one to hold the stilts which governed the angle of the plough blade, and one with a whip to drive the oxen. Because of the irregularities of the land the strips would not all run in the same direction. Some would be at right angles to the majority of strips and some irregularities in the shape of the strips would occur. These odd shaped strips were called "butts" and the pathways left to give access to the strips were called "balks." The oxen would, have been strong and fit for the autumn ploughing after feeding well all summer but the spring ploughing, after the scanty rations of the winter, was hard on both man and beast.

The number of cattle, sheep and pigs the manor could carry would be limited by the small amount of grass that was cultivated. Most of the grass available was the coarse grass which grew in the water meadows alongside streams and rivers or in the poorer soil, known as moors, which were left as common grasslands around the cultivated fields. In the period between September and February there would be two areas of stubble available for pasture; between February and May the cattle had only one field to graze on until Old May Day when traditionally the cattle were turned into the fresh grass on the commons, where they stayed until after the harvest. Each measure of arable land had a recognized amount of common land allotted to it known as "the appurtenances" of the land. The common land in Hornsea bordered the Mere from Foss Dyke, which formed the boundary with Southorpe, eastward around the Mere, running either side of the Seaton Road. Fair Place is the last remaining part of this common land.

Some idea of the number of livestock at this time which a Holderness manor could support on this common land can be obtained from a dispute over grazing rights in North Skirlaugh and Arnold in the 12th century. The jury of the dispute decided that each oxgang of land could sustain in the pasture of the two villages 8 cows and 20 sheep; 4 pigs with their offspring of one year; 4 chickens and one goose with their offspring of one year.

Markets and Fairs

Hornsea was by 1203 one of the four wealthiest manors in Holderness according to the figures given in the Thraves Tax for that year. (A thrave was 24 sheaves). The manors of Hornsea, Humbleton, Swine and Patrington paid the largest amount of tax that year; all four of these manors belonged to the Church.

By the year 1257 Hornsea had become a trading centre and the Abbey of St. Mary's was granted the right to hold a weekly market on Wednesdays. This right, given by Royal Charter, was highly prized for it gave the lord of the manor the right to levy a toll on the produce. The site of this market was traditionally around the stone cross which stood then in the roadway at the junction of Market Place, Southgate and Newbegin.

Some idea of the type of produce sold at this market can be gathered from the details of a complaint made in 1274 by the townspeople of Hornsea against the severity of the tolls levied by the Abbot of St. Mary's at the market. The evidence in the Hundred Rolls reads that the Abbot:-

"...exceeded his liberty by an excess of tolls on

corn, wheat and barley of one farthing, and by
one farthing for an ox and horse hide, and one
farthing for a sheep skin and for a horse with
his load one farthing; and takes chiminage."

(This was payment for passage through woods and forests.)

It would seem from this list that trade at this period was mainly
in the produce of the surrounding manors. The Abbot of the day was
determined to extract as much income from the town as possible for he
was at the same time accused of extorting very high rents from the
townspeople:-

"The villeins of the said abbot distrain within
the bounds of Hornesse for their dwellings as
if they were burgesses of the lord the king and
this has been done three years being elapsed."

The penalties for defying these unjust demands varied from being
put in the pillory, tied to a ducking stool, flung into prison to being
hanged. All these punishments were without warrant the jury decided
and in 1280 a writ was issued against the abbot.

The prosperity and trade of the town steadily increased, for in
1359 Edward III granted to the Abbot of St. Mary's the right to hold two
fairs, one on the 13th August and one on 17th December. These fairs
were held on the common land on the Mereside which is still known
today as "Fair Place." By 1377 Hornsea with Hornsea Beck and Hornsea
Burton had become the fifth largest settlement in the East Riding with
670 inhabitants wealthy enough to pay poll tax. The four larger towns
were Beverley, Hull, Cottingham and Hedon. One reason for the
expansion and prosperity of the town may have been the establishment
of a leather trade in the area; in Sigglesthorne for example, an annual
fair started in 1377 which had mainly leather goods for sale.

Finally, in 1466 the right to hold a weekly market on Thursdays
was granted to the Abbey. There is an unsubstantiated tradition that
the site of this market is marked by the stone cross that stands in
Southgate and that the people of Hornsea Burton and Southorpe used
to sell their produce there.

The Church

The church which existed at the time of Domesday Book was
probably a very simple building with a timber framework covered with
plaster made from a mixture of mud and straw and having a thatched
roof. Some parts of the cobble walls of the present building were built
during the next two centuries, but the major part dates from the end of
the 14th century when St. Mary's rebuilt the Church. In default of any
suitable stone for building, the boulders or cobbles from nearby patches
of boulder clay were used. There may have been an inland deposit of

these boulders but the most likely source would be the beach and cliffs. For the years the church was in building the string of oxen or horses bringing stone from the beach to the site of the church must have been a regular feature of Hornsea life. The very large boulders to be seen at the base of the walls must have needed a sledge of some description to move them. The new church, like several along the coast, was dedicated to St. Nicholas, the patron saint of sailors, mariners and travellers. The rebuilding of the church began in the prosperous time of the 14th Century when the Rector of Hornsea was presumably a wealthy and important figure in the diocese; William de Melton, Rector from 1301 to 1317, was later Archbishop of York. However, when the church was completed in 1422 the Abbey appropriated the Rectory and instituted the Vicarage of Hornsea with a very much diminished income.

The Town

The newly built cobble church standing on the hill above the Market Place would look down onto a small town of single storied cottages, for the most part with mud walls, though with a minority perhaps built of cobbles; all of the cottages would have thatched roofs. The average house at this time was built with a timber frame plastered over with mud and having neither window nor chimney. The only light came from the open doorway during the day, and at night time from primitive lamps made from rushes floating in small bowls of tallow fat, or from the light of the fire. The only escape for the smoke from the open hearth would be by means of a hole in the thatched roof above and to one side of the hearth. It was only in a cobble built cottage that a chimney stack could be constructed.

Apart from the church, the only other sizeable buildings in the town would have been the old Rectory, or Parsonage, which was situated to the north of the church, and the newly built Vicarage which stood in Newbegin in front of the site of the present Vicarage. The Rectory was probably built of cobbles, and was surrounded by a moat; this moat is now incorporated into the hazards of the Hall Garth golf course. After the institution of the Vicarage. the Abbot's Bailiff may have lived in the Rectory. The Vicarage might have been partly built with cobbles but from details in the clerical accounts of the time there seem to have been some parts with mud walls. The Abbey had built the Vicarage which, according to the ordinance, had a hall, a chamber and a kitchen and had a stable and garden together with some enclosed land. The Vicarage did possess one refinement, however, in having a window in the hall, in the clerical accounts this is referred to

"For mending one window in the hall 3d
Anthony Thompson for the sawn waynskot for the window lod"

The particulars of the repairs to the Vicarage given in these accounts contains the following details of the repair of the roof:-

"|tem For reeds for thatching — 2s
For the drawyng of the same — 3d
For thatching of the same — 3d
For the nails that were purchased — 2d
For one clay wall — 6d"

Further items of the accounts indicated how the mud walls were made:-

"|tem Payd Thomas Hyk for wallying 3 days — 13d
For a cart full of stray (straw) — 18d
For 1 laydd (load) of hay of W. Hubilday — 16d
For lyme 1 schowld and a halff — 6s"

The clay was mixed with chopped up straw and then with lime to make a mortar which was then spread over the wooden framework of the walls. The wood for the repairs seems to have been brought in by boat to Hornsea Beck judging from the entry, "For two coupyll spars bought from Hull brig 10d". There were few stands of timber in Holderness, although one of these is identified in the details of the repairs to Riston chapel, which was also the responsibility of the Hornsea Vicar, "For the men of Riston for carriage of wood from Risse Wodde 10d".

Other features of the town which still exist today were the trees in the graveyard, for the sale of wood from the cemetery yielded 16d to the vicar; and the area now called Hall Garth Park was then, as now, a grass enclosure for "... to leasing the Kerke garth to Thoma Pekeryng" gave another 16d rent.

The town would be built around Eastgate, Westgate, Newbegin, Southgate and the Market Place and it is possible that Eastgate and Westgate were the first streets to be settled. The evidence for this comes from the entries in the Manor Court Rolls where many of the cottages in Eastgate and Westgate, which of course bordered the East Field and the West Field, are described as "being a boon" or sometimes "being half a boon". The word "boon" was still used in East Riding dialect until the end of the 19th Century and it meant "to be ready", it seems to have been derived from the Old Norse word "buinn". The "boon" dwellings were held from the Lord of the Manor by the villeins of the manor who in return had to give so many days service on the lord's land each year. There are very few "boon" cottages mentioned in the Manor Court Rolls in Newbegin and Southgate or in the Market Place and of course the name Newbegin seems to indicate a later development.

The broad shape of the Market Place probably developed from the need for a large enclosure to pen the cattle, sheep and pigs offered for sale on market days. It would also have been used to pen the large number of animals run by the tenants of the manor on the common pasture at the time of the yearly count, when a check was made on the number of cattle to prevent overstocking. On market days stalls would be erected around the market cross to display the goods for sale. In the churchyard near the cross stood the stocks in which anyone attempting to sell short weight or rotten goods would be fastened and later pelted with rotten eggs or putrid fish by the villagers.

Outside the town were the hamlets of Northorpe and Southorpe; Southorpe was most probably the "Torp" mentioned in the Domesday entry and Northorpe may have developed as a very small hamlet subsequently.

Thanks to the details for the years 1481 to 1490 gathered by the Vicar, William Otwey, and preserved amongst the documents of the York diocese, the extent and size of the parish are known. Otwey gave the number of his parishioners as follows:-

"First |n Hornsse town   XVII^{xx} and more (340)
|n Hornsse Bek town   XI^{xx} (240)
|n Burton town   50 people
|n Southrope town   30 people
|n Northrope town   14 people
|n Riston town   160 people
|n Arnold town   80 people
|n the Manor of Wodhouse 9 or 10 people"

At the same time Otwey described the extent of his parish:-

"The cure of the seid vicarage fyrst Hornsse Town, Hornsee Bek, halff a myle from the kyrke, Burton halff a myle from the kyrke, Northrope not halff a myle from the Kyrke, Ryston iiii myle from the kyrke, the manor off Wodhous v myle from the kyrke. The nummer off all personnes withyn the paryschynge by estimacion is betwyx xiiii^{cli} (1400) and xv^{cti}(1500) or mo."

The Vicar was trying to establish the need to raise the income of the vicarage and sought to show that the size of his parish warranted an increase. At the same time the names of the tithe payers were given and this is of interest because some of the names are still to be found in Hornsea: Roberto Calyngerth, Willelmo Skelton, Jacob Wilson, Johanne Relfe, Willelme Gemlyng (de Northrope), Johanne Hunter, Petro Loyne, Robert Berear, Ricardo Olyver, Johanne Owbryg, Thomo Mody, Ricardo Hobson, Johanne Stutfield, Willelmo Hykke, Edward Strongbow, Willelmo Skerleygh.

Tithe Disputes

When the vicarage was instituted in 1422, the income was to be derived from the tithes of wool, sheep, flax, hemp, pigs, geese, chickens, eggs, doves, onions, leeks and garden fruits; that is to say one tenth of the value of these products of the parish of Hornsea would be given to the Vicar as part of his income. There were also to be two oxgangs of glebe land to be farmed by, or on behalf of, the Vicar, and the same tithes and amount of glebe land were to be his from the Riston manor. Out of this income the Vicar had to pay the wage of a chaplain at Riston, and be responsible for repairs to the chapel at Riston and to the Hornsea vicarage. The total income of the Vicar was calculated in the deed of ordination to be worth 40 marks or £26. 13s.4d.

In 1493 the vicar of Hornsea, William Otwey, began a suit for an increase to the income of the vicarage in the York Consistory Court against the Abbey of St. Mary's. From the accounts it seems that the tithes and the land in Hornsea did not produce the expected income. The Riston tithes and land produced amounts ranging from between £10 to £15 a year but the Hornsea income was never more than £4 or £5 a year, although at this time Hornsea had a population more than double that of Riston. It may be that disease in Hornsea was the reason for this shortfall; certainly John Wod, Vicar in 1481, stated that in that year no tithe of sheep was received "because of accident". That there had been a drastic reduction in the number of cattle in Hornsea can be gathered from an old man, one of Otwey's witnesses, who could remember when four men of the parish owned more cattle and sheep than all the Hornsea parishioners together in 1493.

As was usual in those days Otwey had to pay a pension to his predecessor, John Wod, from the Hornsea income, and also a pension of 5 marks (£3. 6s. 8d) to a precentor of Beverley Minister from the Riston income. This custom of paying retiring clergy secured them a small income for the remainder of their lives. With these pensions and a large number of repairs to be done to the vicarage, Otwey certainly seemed to have a good case to make for an increase to his income especially as he calculated that the Abbey was receiving an annual income of £60 from the rectorial tithes and land in Hornsea over the same period.

In the accounts of Otwey's income the tithes are mixed in with his fees for the religious duties he performed and read very curiously: 5 ducks 10d; 38 chickens 2s; 18 pigs 3s. 9d; 6 doves 2d; apples and pears 8d; leeks and onions 1d; honey and wax 3d; flax and hemp 7s. 6d; for 5 weddings 20d; for 3 funerals 18d; churchings 3s. 9d; eggs 3s.

The tithes were calculated and collected for the vicar by a bailiff, usually one of the parishioners; at Riston for instance, "Thoma Benit paid 4d for collecting the tithes." Although the amounts received from the garden produce seem pathetically small, the right to tithe would have been lost to any future incumbent if they had not been collected.

In spite of these detailed accounts Otwey was unable to secure a favourable verdict, for the Judge in the Consistory Court found for the

Abbey and dismissed his suit. Otwey was so outraged at this injustice that he determined to publicly show defiance of the Abbey. In 1494 on the afternoon of Easter Sunday, the holiest day in the Christian calendar, he took out the Abbot's boats and nets in broad daylight and in full view of the parish, and went fishing for bream and pike in the Mere, thus infringing upon the Abbey's most highly prized privilege. For this defiance he was excommunicated but presumably, after due penance, was restored to his living, for he remained vicar until 1499.

SAINT NICHOLAS' CHURCH
(About 1785)
This engraving shows the church as it looked before the
Victorian restoration of the mid-19th century. The main walling
material is cobble, as, in the Middle Ages, it was prohibitively
expensive to import large amounts of quarried stone from inland.
Much of the interior dates from the 14th and 15th centuries. The
church originally had a wooden spire which was a noted sea
mark on the coast. The spire blew down in 1714.

3 The Guilds and Guildhouses in Hornsea

The first guilds seem to have originated in Anglo-Saxon times. Most probably they were brought into being for the protection and mutual aid of their members during the evolution of the feudal system. On entering the guilds an oath of membership was taken which gave a man freedom to attend the periodical meetings in a guildhouse or hall; these meetings were always occasions for heavy drinking. Members also contributed towards a central treasury which could be drawn upon by a guildsman in cases of misfortune such as ill health or fire, etc., thus giving a form of insurance.

After the Norman Conquest the guilds came to be primarily associated with religious occasions and many of the guilds, now named after a patron saint, were mainly concerned with the organizing of the religious processions which were held on saints' days and other holy days of the church.

From the middle of the 13th century the number of guilds increased enormously. This was mainly due to the development of the craft guilds. These guilds aimed at protecting the standards of workmanship of a particular craft as well as providing the good fellowship and mutual aid of the Saxon guilds. The standards of workmanship laid down by the guild members were enforced by two "searchers and tryers" chosen by the guild; bad workmanship could lead to a fine set by the court steward at the guild court. The tradition of "searchers and tryers" was taken over by the manor courts, after the guilds were suppressed in 1546, when ale tasters, searchers of yarn, flesh greaves and bread and butter weighers could be appointed by the courts.

An example of the type of aid which the guilds would give to members can be seen in the ordinance of the Guild of Holy Trinity, Hull which ordained in April 1369:-

> "A revenue for the guild of two shillings of silver to be raised at four times of the year at the Feast of the Nativity of John (June), St. Michael (September), The Nativity of Our Lord and Easter. If any of the Brothers and Sisters languishes in a perpetual infirmity so that they have not of their own to support themselves we ordain that such infirm man or

woman shall take every week of the goods of
the said Guild eight pence and at the Feast of
St. Martin in Winter one tunic and a little
cap."

Importance was attached by the guilds to the details of the
funeral ceremonies, for instance, the number of candles and tapers
burnt and the number of masses said on the death of a member.

In the 14th century Beverley was an important medieval town, far
larger than Hull, and had altogether 38 guilds associated with a large
number of crafts, the names of which help to give an idea of town life at
that time. They included mercers, drapers, tanners, masons, skinners,
tailors, goldsmiths, smiths, plumbers, bowlers, turners, girdlers,
cutlers, horners, spooners, weavers, fullers, cartwrights, coverlet
weavers, arrow makers, bowyers, bakers, butchers, fishmongers,
chandlers, barbers, vintners, saddlers, ropers, hairers, shipmen and
glovers.

One of the founder members of the Holy Trinity guild in Hull was
a Thomas de Hornsea and his wife; this guild was always associated
with mariners and was known as the shipmen's guild. The first
documentary evidence of the existence of the guilds in Hornsea lies in
the will of the last rector of Hornsea, Anthony St. Quintin, who died in
1422. In his will he left 10s. to each of the four guilds in Hornsea
Church; Corpus Christi, St. Mary, St. Catherine and Holy Trinity.
Hornsea was at this time the fifth largest settlement in the East Riding;
some 670 people in the town of Hornsea with Hornsea Beck and
Hornsea Burton were rich enough to pay poll tax in 1377. The four
guilds of Hornsea can be compared with nearby Bridlington which had
at that time only two.

Apart from Holy Trinity it is not possible to derive any precise
connection between one craft and one guild. However there are two
references in records to St. Mary's as the weavers' guild. It is possible
that all four Hornsea guilds were solely religious and charitable in
nature.

In 1528 Robert Metham, bailiff for the Abbey of St. Mary's, left in
his will a quarter of barley to the four guilds in Hornsea church;
presumably this would be used to brew beer for the guild members. The
guilds as religious institutions were suppressed by Edward VI in 1549.
In a list of properties taken over afterwards by the Crown, which was
drawn up in 1556, is mention of a ring belonging to the guilds of
Hornsea. According to the evidence of the Vicar of Hornsea, John
Rogers, this ring, with a stone in it, was in the custody of the curate of
the guild who used it to cure people of eye diseases. Further details of
the alleged curative powers of the ring were given by Robert Coneston,
yeoman, who said that the stone of the ring, which was only little, did
much good to those with eye diseases. Apparently the ring was delivered
to a man called Bellows who plucked out the stone with his bodkin and

put it in his purse. This same Bellows had also, "... taken a drinking horn worth 7 nobles pretending that it belonged to the guild in Hornsea which in fact belonged to Richard Robinson of Hornsea who had it made and used to lend it to the guild." This episode highlights the superstitious beliefs of the age and confirms the importance of drinking in the guild fellowship.

A seal belonging to the guild of St. Catherine was dug up near the Church during building repairs in 1868. This guild also owned land in the Hornsea East Field, for in 1658, "... fower butts and the appurtenances neere Northorpe belonging to Saint Catherine Guild," figure in a transaction in the Manor Court Rolls.

The Guildhouses

Although there were four guilds in Hornsea, there are references to only three guildhouses in the Manor Court Rolls, in Newbegin, Southgate and Westgate. It may have been that two guilds shared the use of one house, although it may have been that a guildhouse once stood at Hornsea Beck. Holy Trinity, the mariners' guild, may have had a guildhouse amongst the fishermen and sailors who lived there. Some 38 houses had been destroyed by sea erosion between 1546 and 1608; the Manor Court Rolls date only from 1625. Two of the three guildhouses, those in Southgate and Westgate, were built on hills; there is constant reference to the guildhouse hill in the entries.

The first reference to the Newbegin guildhouse is in 1671:- "... one house, called the Guilds house and garth in Newbegine," and there follow references to the house until the end of the Manor Court Rolls in 1814. In 1746 it passed into the possession of a widow, Peace Bedell, and subsequently to a John Bedell. This John Bedell was an exciseman and the father of E.W. Bedell who published in 1848, "An Account of Hornsea." In 1805, "... a cottage in Newbegin called Guild House together with three cottages lately built there on," was sold and this is followed in 1807 by an entry which helps to identify the site:-

> "The dwelling house lately erected upon a parcel of a cottage in Newbegin called by the name of Guild House and the Garth thereto together with the Yard and Garden and all that garth containing by estimation two roods lying on the South side or back side of the said three several tenements."

Newbegin runs roughly in an East to West direction and all the houses are built directly on the street line; the mention of the garth lying on the, "... south side or back side," of the house means that the house must lie on the south side of Newbegin. According to the map of 1864 there are only two portions of land on the south side large enough to be 2 roods or 2,420 square yards in size, and only one of these has a building on it. It is the house which was afterwards called Tower House.

The last owner of the property knew that the father of E.W. Bedell had lived there which helps to confirm the identification.

The guildhouse in Southgate is first mentioned in the Manor Court Rolls in 1651 when, "... a cottage neare Gildouss hill," was sold, and later, in 1688, "... a cottage in Southgate called Gildhall House," was sold to a George Barnes. There is no further reference to the Gildhall House after this and it may have been pulled dawn afterwards. However the site is still referred to as Gildas Hill until 1718, when the sale is recorded of, "... a cottage in Southgate near Gildas Hill commonly called White House with the yard and out houses thereof belonging to the beck thereof." The beck was the stream now called Stream Dyke and it would seem from this that the White House lay alongside the beck. In 1719 Francis Coulson surrendered part of the garth of the Whitehouse from the North West corner, "... fronting the street." This shows that the White House was on the East side of Southgate and the entry in 1722 of, "... a cottage in Southgate near Gildas Hill commonly called White House and two cottages adjoining upon Football Green," place the White House as being on the land now used as a cemetery in Southgate; the highest point on this land lies just East of the cross in Southgate and this is possibly the site of the guildhouse.

There are no references to a guildhouse or hall being in Westgate but repeated references to a cottage near "Gildhill." By careful study of the entries in the Manor Court Rolls it is possible to eliminate all of the cottages on the South side of Westgate and some of those on the North side. The remaining area, a sloping bank which is now occupied by Westgate House and the land immediately to the west of it, is most probably the "Gildhill."

In view of the aims of the guilds, the subsequent history of the three sites is interesting. Tower House in Newbegin was pulled down in 1966 and a home for the elderly was built there by the East Riding County Council. The Southgate "Gildas Hill" is part of the land bought by the Hornsea Local Board of Health in 1885 for a cemetery, a mortuary chapel being built at the entrance. Finally, Westgate House was converted into a home for the elderly in 1955 by Hull Corporation.

4 Hornsea Beck and Hornsea Burton

Hornsea Beck

Over the centuries several villages which once existed on the coast of Holderness have been washed away by the sea. The low clay cliffs of this part of the coast offer little resistance to the waves, and land is constantly being eroded at a rate of some 2½ yards or more each year. One of the lost villages of Holderness was the small port and fishing village of Hornsea Beck which took its name from the beck or stream which flowed from the Mere to the sea.

There is no mention of this village in Domesday Book and it may not have been in existence then. However, details of a dispute in 1228 over the will of a Walter Spiney show that a small port or landing place was established by that date. This dispute was over the rights to tithe the profits of the boats landing at Hornsea port. As Lord of the Manor of Hornsea the Abbey of St. Mary's, York, was awarded the right to tithe boats landing to the North of the beck or stream; those landing on the South of the stream paid tithes to the Lord of the Seigniory of Holderness. As part of the settlement of this dispute the Abbey of St. Mary's agreed to maintain the pier and harbour.

The stream, also known rather confusingly as the beck, ran at that time in a more North-Easterly direction than it does now for the last half of its journey from the Mere to the sea. There seems, according to several old maps, to have been a projecting spit of land to the south of the outlet of this stream; presumably this gave a sheltered anchorage to small fishing boats on what was otherwise an exposed stretch of coast. The port of Hornsea Beck flourished over the years. It was listed as a port in Hollinshed in 1400, and by 1485 had some 240 inhabitants compared with 340 at that time in nearby Hornsea. A wooden quay or key as it was usually spelt, had been built to safeguard the harbour, but by the beginning of the 16th century this was in a very dilapidated state. According to evidence given in a tithe dispute in 1555:-

> *"The said Key of Hornesey about 30 or 40 years ago was once and again in great ruin and the Abbot and Convent put off the repair of the same for a long time on account of the great expense necessary."*

The fishermen of the town, realising that their livelihood was at stake, hit upon the idea of giving an extra "dolles or cadolles" of fish, the equivalent of, "... a mans ryght of fyshe of every shypp of the parish belonging to the sayd Key for every tyme that the sayd shypp goeth furthe a fysshyng," hoping by this extra payment to move the Abbot to repair the Key.

However, the damage to the Key was so extensive that the repairs were not undertaken by the Abbey. After the dissolution of the monasteries the Manor of Hornsea passed into the possession of the Crown. Appeals for help with the rebuilding of the Key were sent to the Privy Council in 1549; in letters to the Earl of Shrewsbury was:-

> *"... a platt sent by Richard Mansell of Hornsey Beck, declaring the pere to be ruyned whereby the King lost certain yerely rentes, his Lordship must send thither summe man of skill to consider what stuff is there towards the reparacion of the pere and what more shall be nedefull and what may be the charges thereof."*

Both the money and the advice were given proved to be inadequate to repair all the damage for in 1553 another payment was authorized:-

> *"Mr. Chauncellour to direct out his warrant for the diffrayment of £1,000 more than the other thousand poundes that hath byn by the ordre of the King's Majestie all ready bestowed about the peere of Hornsey so as the woorkes may be fynished out of hande."*

It may have been the materials sent in response to this second appeal for help which figured in an action by the Crown Commissioners against a man called Bellows when in 1556 he was accused of, "... carrying away to his house at Grimsby about 20 tons and two little pieces of timber which was for the repair of Hornsea Pier."

Even when the pier was repaired it proved impossible to stay the inroads of the sea; each year more and more land was washed away and in a very few years the pier was again in a state of ruin. At an inquisition, held in 1609, into the question of rebuilding the pier at Hornsea it was said that since 1546 a total of 38 houses had been washed away by the sea together with a 240 yards wide strip of land along the coast. It was calculated at this inquisition that £3,000 would be needed to rebuild the pier and in view of the fate of the previous pier, not surprisingly, no further action was taken.

Some remnant of the projecting spit of land at Hornsea Beck is shown on a map of 1610 and in the Manor Court Rolls several cottages at Hornsea Beck were still being surrendered in the latter part of the 17th century. However the last entry of any property at Hornsea Beck comes in 1744 and by 1785 a map drawn that year by J. Tuke marks the, "Site of the Town of Hornsea Beck" as being under the sea.

Measuring from the present coastline the site of Hornsea Beck lies now about a quarter of a mile off shore, about 200 yards north of the present Marine Hotel.

Hornsea Burton

"Burtune" in the "Soke of Hornesse" containing two carucates of ploughland was part of the lands given by William the Conqueror to Drogo de la Beuvrière in 1066. After Drogo became an outlaw in 1085 "Burtune" passed to Odo, Count of Champagne and after his rebellion against William Rufus it finally passed to William le Gros, Count of Aumale, Lord Seigniory of Holderness.

William le Gros, (the Fat,) had taken a vow to go on pilgrimage to Jerusalem and to release him from this vow he was obliged to give land to the Cistercian order of monks. Part of this gift of land was used to help found Meaux Abbey in 1150.

The abbey seems during the next eighty years to have become bankrupt twice, the first time due to the heavy ransom raised throughout England for the release of Richard I. On the second occasion some of the monks were received by the Priory of Bridlington. The abbey re-opened in 1220 and in 1245 the Abbot Michael obtained the gift of 45 acres of land in Hornsea Burton from the then Count of Aumale.

About this time too, Bridlington Priory was given two oxgangs of land (about 30 acres) by the Count, and a "Henry de Spineto" gave three tofts and their appurtenances in Hornsea Burton to Bridlington Priory as well.

There were five tenants in Hornsea Burton in 1297 according to a tax return of that year. They were William of Tickton, William son of Galfrida, Richard's widow, Radulf Groynepork, and Walter's son, Robert. The "town of Hornesse Burtona" entered separately had two tax payers; Willelmus des Espynes, (translated sometimes as William de Spineto, sometimes as William of the Spinney,) and Richard of Tickton.

Later the Fauconberg family held two oxgangs of land in Hornsea Burton and in 1401 Isabel wife of Sir Walter Fauconberg of Catfoss died seized of two oxgangs in Hornsea Burton held of Thomas of Lancaster, (later Duke of Clarence and Earl of Aumale.)

When the smaller monasteries were dissolved in 1536, a survey of their possessions showed that Swine Convent, (also a Cistercian foundation begun at the same time as Meaux Abbey,) held land in, "ye fields of Horynise Burton."

In 1539 Hornsea Burton was leased to Sir Ralph Ellerker who held it of Sir John Fynes. He was followed by his son, also Sir Ralph, who died in 1546. The next record of "Hornesey Burton" is in Jacobean times when it passed to John Egerton and his wife Anne, who held it between 1603 and 1614.

The fields of Hornsea Burton were enclosed in 1663 and on a map of the awards is shown a post mill standing in Mill Lane. There were 460 acres awarded amongst eight people, one of whom was Oliver Kitteridge, a Quaker.

Until 1785, when the beck from the Mere was straightened and channelled into its present course and became known subsequently as Stream Dyke, the land between Mill Lane and the beck would be waterlogged and difficult to cultivate and it would be here that Hornsea Burton Mere, mentioned in 1280, would form in wet weather.

It is not possible to know definitely where the common land of Hornsea Burton was. It may have been along the cliff edge on land long since eroded. On the other hand, it may have stretched along the boundary with Southorpe, marked by Foss Dyke, to Rolston Road and Southgate. There has been for many years a huge stone at the junction of Hull Road and Southgate which might have marked such a pre-enclosure boundary.

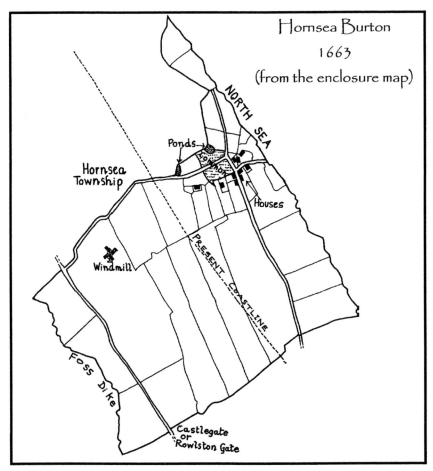

Hornsea Burton

1663

(from the enclosure map)

5 The Manor of Hornsea in the 17th and 18th Centuries

The Lord of the Manor

The Manor of Hornsea had been administered by a Master of the Manors as part of the large estate owned by the Abbey of St. Mary's, York, with a Bailiff supervising the minor details of working the land and collecting the rectorial tithes. The manor lands, the Old Rectory or Parsonage north of the church and the rectorial tithes were, after the dissolution of the monasteries, taken over by the Crown in 1538 and subsequently all three properties had a very chequered history, often under separate owners.

All three items remained Crown property until 1553 when Sir Richard Blunt, a "Gentleman of the Privie Chamber," was granted a 21 years lease of, "... the parsonage of Hornesey with one close of ground there called Hallgarth." It may be that the manorial lands were leased at the same time by the Constables of Burton Constable for, in 1557 title to the Seigniory of Holderness passed to them. Certainly in 1572 when, as a Catholic recusant, Sir Robert Constable was fined in the reign of Queen Elizabeth I, the "Manor of Hornesey with Hornesey Burton," was one of twenty properties which contributed to the fine. Ten years later in 1582 the same properties are listed when Sir Robert was again fined heavily as was "Robert Foukes." The Foukes or Fawkes family, who were also Catholics, have a special place in English history.

The impropriator of the rectorial tithes was responsible for the repair of the chancel of Hornsea church, as had been the Abbey before the dissolution of the monasteries. In 1575, by the evidence of a churchwarden's complaint, a Mr. John Armitage had purchased the right to the rectorial tithes. In 1597 the Manor had passed to the Moore family and in 1611 this family bought the Rectory House from a Michael Wharton. The Wharton family had also acquired the right to the rectorial tithes.

By 1625 the manor had reverted to the Crown according to the evidence of the Manor Court Rolls where the preamble to the entries runs, "... surrenders unto the hands of our Sovaraigne Lord the King." After the Civil War came the establishment of the Commonwealth in 1649 and the Manor of Hornsea was taken over by Parliament. The preamble in April 1649 includes, "... unto the hands of the Kepyrs of the Liboorties of England by Authority of Parliament, Lords of this Mannor." The Steward of the Court seems to have been writing in a state of some confusion for, after twice using the new wording, he relapses into the old title, "... our Sovaraigne Lord the King," for the next two entries. At the Michaelmas Manor Court in October that year he again gets confused and has eight new titles in the preamble followed by two old ones.

In 1650 and 1651 the Manor was leased to Sir Robert Borwick who is described in the Manor Court Rolls as, "... Trustee appointed by Parliament." From 1651 to 1659 it was leased to three people together, William Spencer, Francis Lewis and William Micklay. From 1659 to 1660 William Spencer and William Micklay were joint lessees. Meanwhile the Old Rectory House was sold to Peter Acklam in 1651 by Robert Moore.

The restoration of the monarchy in June 1660 led to the manor returning to the Crown, a fact announced with a Latin inscription in a new and flowing handwriting in the Manor Court Rolls. In 1662 King Charles II married Catherine of Braganza and in 1670 he gave the Manor of Hornsea to his wife. For the next four years the preamble reads, "... unto the hands of our Sovereigne lady the Queene being Ladie of this Manor."

From 1674 to 1680 Sir Hugo and Slingsby Bethell jointly leased the Manor; then for the next four years Slingsby Bethell was the sole lessee. From 1684 to 1760 the Quaker family, the Acklams, held the manor and finally in 1760 William Bethell became, by purchase, owner of the manor and in this family the title of Lord of the Manor of Hornsea remains today.

The Manor Court

Before 1538 the Manor Court would probably have been held in the Rectory, or Parsonage, which stood north of the church. The Master of the Manors of the Abbey would be representing the Lord of the Manor, the Abbot. The Abbot's Bailiff would provide the details of the produce of the Manor from the Abbey lands and from the land leased to the tenants. After 1538, at times when the various lessees of the manor were not resident in the town, the Manor Court may have been held in one of the two inns.

The title of the Manor Court in the 17th Century Court Rolls is given at the beginning of each court as, "The View of Frankpledge and Customary Court for Copyholders." Frankpledge was a system dating from Anglo-Saxon times whereby all those over 14 years of age were required to belong to a group called a "tithing." Each person in the tithing was obliged to be responsible for the good behaviour of everyone else in the group, or communal penalties would ensue. The View of Frankpledge was a meeting held to check that all those eligible were in a tithing. By the 17th century the enforcement of Frankpledge had become largely traditional. The "Customary Court" was held to enforce the "custumal," which was a written record of the customs of the manor. This became in time the court for the copyholders of the land. The copyholders were the successors of the Medieval villeins. In theory, they were only given the temporary ownership of land by the Lord of the Manor. The authority for their tenure of the land lay in the entry in the Manor Court Rolls of which they held a copy, hence the name. In contrast, freeholders held land or property which was not subject to manorial customs.

Details given in the deeds of some of the old cottages seem to point to an earlier time when the transfer of land was signified by the handing over of a straw in place of a document. The tenant of the land would come to the Manor Court "straw in hand" and give the straw to the Lord of the Manor, or his representative, as representing the land itself. The straw was then passed on to the new tenant. Also from these deeds it seems that the "boon hereditaments," i.e., dwellings established in Medieval times, were expected to pay annually to the Lord of the Manor "two bottins of straw and a peppercorn" as their feudal due. (A bottin or bottle of straw was as much as one person could carry.) Some of the cottages in the Manor Court Rolls were entered as being "two boons" and others as being "half a boon." These payments or their equivalent in cash continued until 1926.

To return to the 17th century, as has been seen, the Customary Court for the copyholders had been established. By the late 18th Century the title of the Court in the Manor Court Rolls had changed to, "The View of Frankpledge with Court Baron and Customary Court." The Court Baron was an assembly of freeholders, who met to enforce the customs of the manor. Thus, by the late 18th century the Hornsea Manor Court dealt with both copyholders and freeholders. The court was held twice a year; in the spring on or near to St. Mark's Day, April 25th and one in the autumn on or near to St. Michael's Day, September 29th.

The Officers of the Court

These were, by the 17th century, the **Lord's Steward** who acted as his representative; the **Steward of the Manor**, usually a lawyer, who acted as the secretary of the court; and the **Bailiff**, who was a local man able to oversee the working of the land and to check the amount harvested. In the 18th Century three of the Lord's Stewards were successively Suckling Spendlove, Marmaduke Prickett and Hassell Moor.

The decisions about the working of the land, the tenancy of property and the inheritance of it on the death of a tenant were made by the jury of the Manor Court or the "hommage" as it was called. The jury, twelve in number, was chosen from among the most respected tenants of the manor. As well as deciding questions of ownership, etc., the jury could set fines for tenants who broke the by-laws of the manor. In other towns records exist, for instance, of fines for letting pigs and geese stray in the lanes of the town, or for breaking down hedges or for failing to clean the ditches which drained the fields. In the surviving records of the Manor Court in Hornsea there is only one reference to a fine being paid. This occurs in 1748, when, "... Robert Hornby being a tenant within this Manor and duly summoned to appear the court has made default therefore he is amerced one shilling."

As well as the jury, several other officers were elected annually. Two **Bylawmen** were chosen to decide when the ploughing of the Hornsea fields should begin and on what date the animals of the village should be turned onto the pasture. A **Pindar** was responsible for supervising the number of cattle and pigs, etc., that each villager had grazing in the fields and common. Each year a count was made and, if any villager was found to have more animals than he was entitled to, the extra animals were penned in the penfold, or pinfold as it was more often called locally. They were kept by the pindar until the fine set by the court was paid. The two officers who decided the amount of fine to be paid were called the **Affeerors**. In Hornsea, before the enclosure of the open fields, the pinfold was in Eastgate near to the gate leading from Eastgate into the East Field. In the Court Rolls in 1744, "... three parcels of a cottage in Eastgate near the pinfold," were surrendered. The three cottages now called "Cedar Cottages" are still there and the pinfold was nearby. Opposite the cottages is the gateway into the East Field still marked by a short lane.

Although Bedell claims that a **Neatherd**, or Nowtherd, as local dialect rendered it, was chosen each year, there is no mention of one in the Manor Court Rolls. The duty of the neatherd was to collect the cattle from the village after the morning milking, lead them out to the fields and then bring them back in the evening. ("Little Boy Blue" was a neatherd immortalised in the nursery rhyme.)

Other officers appointed by the Manor Court were the **Leather Searchers and Tryers** who seem to have been chosen from the mid-17th century to the mid-18th century. Their task was to check the quality of the leather and the workmanship of the goods produced in the town and between two and six were chosen each year. The court also chose two **Constables** whose duty it was to keep the peace at all times, particularly on market days when arguments were liable to break out over the bargaining. Finally for a few years towards the end of the 17th Century an **Ale Finer** was appointed. His duties were to check the quality of the ale sold in the town inns and ale houses.

Certain family names occur over and over again in the members of the jury in the 17th century. The names were often Bonfield, Whitfield, Midforth, Foster, Robinson, Galloway, Acklam and Arksey. In the 18th Century the surnames of the jury were often Jarrat, Usher, Ulliot, Hobson, Tiplady, Wilson, Foster, Burn and Bedell.

The record of the Manor Court business was kept in the Manor Court Rolls. The surviving Manor Court Rolls of Hornsea are in two volumes, one covering the years 1625 to 1769 and the other from 1769 to 1818. Each Court begins with the preamble, e.g., for the court held in 1770:-

> *"To wit the View of Frank Pledge with Court Baron and Customary Court of William Bethell, Esq., Lord of the Manor aforesaid, held at the accustomed Place in and for the said Manor on Wednesday the Eighteenth day of April in the Year of our Lord One Thousand Seven Hundred and Seventy before Suckling Spendlove, Gentleman, Steward of the said Manor."*

Then came the names of the hommage, or jury, usually in three columns of four. Then underneath came the names and titles of the Bylawmen, Pindar, Affeeror, etc. Then came the entries. A typical entry is one relating to the cottage now 36 Southgate in the year 1670:-

> *"To this court cometh Henrie Hornbie, Jo. Boulton, and J. Thompson and surrenders into ye hands of ye Queene being Ladie of this Manor one cottage in Southgate in Hornsea and the appurtenances there to belonging to me the said Henrie and Ellis my wife for our lives naturall and after to Gabriell Hornbie my son and his heirs for ever according to ye custom of this Manor."*

Some idea of the style of the proceedings is given in an entry in 1750:-

> *"That publick proclamation was made by the Bayliff of the said Manor in Open Court that ye heir at law of ye said Jonathan Green should come into Court and make out his claim to be admitted to the Equity of Redemption."*

As well as giving details of the surrender and exchange of properties, the Court Rolls give details of agreements entered into by the jury on behalf of all the tenants of the Manor, for instance in 1745:-

> *"Be it remembered that the inhabitants of Hornsea doth make an agreement with William Purdom of Skipsea to catch and kill all the Moles in Hornsay Fields and Southorp Fields and all the Common Pastures Belonging the said Township of Hornsey and the said William Purdom his to Receive every year for Hornsey Fields and Leys One Pound, for Southorp Fields Twelve shillings for Term of his life if the said William Purdom Catch and Kill them to please the Inhabitants of Hornsea."*

Three years later is another example:-

"*Be it remembered in the year 1748 the inhabitants of the township of hornsay. That is to say the jury at this time whose names are under written Doth agree of a Contract with Thomas Atkinson Joyner and Carpenter to keep and maintain all the Gates, Bridges and Rails in good and sufficient repair belonging the aforesaid Township Except that belongs the Constabulary, for consideration as such he the aforesaid Thomas Atkinson is to have two gates* In Far Field and three in Southorp field and three in hornsay fields. Likewise twenty shillings yearly for the Leys. Also seven shillings and sixpence yearly for the Gates and Rails at Lelley Close End and Rowlston Lane End. But as he Enters upon them much out of Repair for this year only and the aforesaid Thomas Atkinson doth Contract this for life as Witness our hand.*"

*In this context a "gate" is the right of pasture for one animal, and not a barrier.

These agreements seem to give a glimpse of the leading villagers of the small market town carefully bargaining over the interests of the town, helped in their deliberations by the smoking of the long clay pipes of the period, remains of which can still be dug up in cottage gardens.

Interesting Details from the Manor Court Rolls

Whilst the names of the families in the Manor Rolls seemed to change over the years, the names of the cottages and the holdings of land remained the same. One oxgang was held by several owners over 100 years or more, but each time was named in the Rolls as "Old Jerome Midforth's Oxgang." The cottages and closes had very workaday names, such as Gillgrass, Fishhouse Close, (by the Mere landing place,) Killclose Garth, Leek House and Hog Garth, (in Newbegin,) Sugmire and Barnby Garth, (in Eastgate,) Prestwood Close and Dovecote Garth (the site of the Primary School, Newbegin,) and surely the least attractive of all, Hogpit Hall in Newbegin.

The words used to describe the various properties are derived from several languages. The "garth" is an Anglo-Saxon word for a yardlike enclosure around the house, where the rabbit hutches, chicken coops, etc., would be kept. A "croft" meaning a small field or paddock adjoining a dwelling house is Danish, as is a "toft" meaning a house together with a small field. The same property, the toft, can also be called by the Norman name of "messuage" and both words would be used to describe a typical cottage surrounded by a smallholding used as orchard or vegetable garden. The Norman word "close" is used in the Rolls to describe a place surrounded by a fence.

The record of everyday events of the town recorded in the Rolls is occasionally interrupted to show the wider world outside. In 1648, at the time of the Civil War, it is recorded:-

> *"We find Jo. Midforth butcher, heir to Enoch Midforthe of two cottages in Hornesey Fields, if the said Enoch bee dead for he is in the warres and hath not been heard of these five years soe that if hee come noe more we find ye said John next heire to the said premises, and if ye s* Enoche come and be living then he is to injoye the said cottages as in his former estate."*

The Midforth family owned a cottage with a kiln in Southgate and it might have been here, in the incident described in Bedell, that some Parliamenarian troops broached a keg of ale in the street on their journey through the town from Hull to Scarborough. Of another member of the Midforth family it is recorded in 1671, "... that John Midforth departed from the Town of Hornsey to travill about 8 or 9 years and has not been heard of any more." There is also another "John Midforth, soldier," in 1719. It would seem that this family had a tradition of soldiering.

The sort of problem the jury might have to decide when tenants died is shown in an entry in 1686:-

> *"George Richardson the younger dyed seased of five cottages lyeing in footeball greene and in Southgate in hornsey also One oxgang and a halfe of Land Lying in Hornsey Feildes with all and every of their appurtenances their to belonging and that the said George being not compos mentis as we are informed by sceverall Witnesses Who is upon their oathes that hee had Liettel or no Common Scence in him When hee past the estate over to his Mother and theirfore by testamouny and oure owne Judgement wee find James Richardson who is this said George Richardson father brother eldest son next heire."*

In two instances the Rolls are used to record bequests of lands and property. In 1770 a Mary Olds left £10 apiece to half a dozen people, £5 to another group of friends and finally her silver tankard to "John Olds of London." This convivial lady makes a very marked contrast to poor Isabell C— who figures in an entry of 1775:-

"Whereas the said George C— has been a very bad husband to my said daughter. My will is that he shall have no manner of Rights and Trusts to any of my personal or real Estate or surrender of the aforesaid Lands from her. And I do hereby appoint Mr. Will Wilson and Mr. James Moor both of Hornsea Trustees for my aforesaid daughter Isabel C— and desire them to act as such to receive the Rents for her when they become due and to pay them to her and only her and that a receipt from her shall be a sufficient Discharge for them."

There are two cases of property owned by families in 1650 still being in their possession 250 years later. The first instance concerns the Carr family In 1659 George Carr and his wife can take possession of, "... a cott in Nubegine to the use of their heirs for ever with egress and regress throw the garth it being the Southend and if the aforesaid George Carr throwe downe a gappe he shall be at the cost to make it up againe." Later in 1716 is an agreement between Mary Carr widow and the Acklams about a boundary wall "... from the Kitching End North ward to Mr. Acklam's Hall Garths." Rose Carr, a descendent of this family, owned the property in Newbegin at the beginning of the 20th century.

The second example is the Robinson family. In 1651 Leonard Robinson died seized of, "... one house called the Gildhouse in Newbegin, two shops in the Market Place called a cottage and Lelley Close called a cottage." This Leonard Robinson was one of the jury of the Manor Court and George Robinson, his son, was constable in 1670. Successive generations of the Robinson family did duty as officers of the parish and manor throughout the next 150 years. Lelley Close was in Lelley Lane, the old name for Hull Road. The Robinson family were still living in a cobble cottage, now rebuilt as Field House, at the turn of the 20th century.

The Manor Court was still functioning up until 1818 when entries in the Rolls finish several years after the Enclosures. After that time the Steward of the Manor Court was elected annually. Bulmer's Directory of East Yorkshire, published in 1892, lists the Steward and the Bailiff amongst the officials of the town. The Court dinner was still being held annually in one of the hotels up until 1910.

6 Village Trades

Before the enclosure of the open fields and the Industrial Revolution, Hornsea people, like most of the Holderness villagers, relied on food grown in their fields for their staple diet. The wool, flax and leather produced locally also served to provide them with clothing. The markets and fairs were responsible for the introduction of more exotic foodstuffs, etc., but these would be too expensive for everyday life.

Tanning

The constant need for supplies of leather for shoes, gloves, jerkins and breeches, as well as harness and saddles, meant that Hornsea, like most small towns, had a thriving tanyard. The curing of the leather, which transformed the raw hides into the different types of leather, needed a constant supply of running water. Water pits some 7 feet square would be built on the sides of a stream and here the raw hides would be left to soak for a week. Then any blood left on the hide would be removed by scrubbing. The hides had next to have the hair from the outer side and a layer of fat on the inside removed. This was achieved by first loosening these unwanted tissues by soaking the hides in three successive lime pits, using slaked lime solution in increasing strengths. Leather for soles was left to soak for10 days, harness leather for 12 to 14 days and upper shoe leather needed 6 weeks soaking. The hides were then placed on a wooden beam or "horse" as it was called and the loosened hair scraped off. This hair was stored and sold to plasterers as one of the constituents of plaster. Next, a very sharp, double edged knife was used to remove the layer of inner fat or "fleshings." This fat was also retained and later boiled down for tallow for candles. Cow hides were then given a final wash with a weak acid solution but calf hides and sheep skins needed further treatment. The latter were put into "mastering" pits which had a mixture of cold water with either hen dung or pigeon dung and were left there for 10 to 12 days before receiving their final wash in an acid solution.

The hides had now to be tanned. This was achieved by using a mixture of oak bark, ground to a fine powder, and cold water in a series of ten leeching pits containing increasingly strong mixtures of oak bark and water. After the tannin of the bark had tanned the hides they were removed from the leeching pits and washed and dried. The final stage was to rub a thin layer of oil over the leather to prevent complete drying out and consequent cracking. Then the leather was hung out of the sunlight in a dark room until needed.

In Hornsea in the 17th Century the leather trade was of sufficient importance to warrant the appointment of leather feelers and leather tryers by the Manor Court from 1667 onwards. The parish register lists the occupations of the deceased for this period too, and this shows that a third of the occupations were connected with the leather trade, e.g., glover, tanner, cordwainer, currier, saddler and skinner. It is possible that leather goods were marketed in the 14th and 15th centuries, for in the neighbouring village of Sigglesthorne, a fair for the sale of leather ware was held each autumn in the 14th Century. This trade might also explain the second market day granted in 1446. The market was probably held around the cross in Southgate, and near the Hornsea tanyard. This tanyard is described in an entry in the Manor Court Rolls as being, "... all that cottage with Barns and stables, buildings and other outhouses belonging and adjoining together with the Tanyard, Orchards, Garth and Beckside," and was situated on the Beck north of Southgate. Many of the leather workers lived in cottages nearby. For example, Francis Coulson, glover, lived at the Whitehouse, and Robert Willson, breeches maker and William Stork, cordwainer, lived in Southgate. Breeches were often made of leather in those days for hard wear and were worn with a smock over them. A cordwainer worked with the finer types of leathers imported originally from Cordova in Spain. Finally, as evidence of a thriving leather trade, the tithes listed in 1764 have rape as one of the tithe payments. This plant was cultivated for the oil obtained by crushing the seed, and it was this oil which was used in the final stage of preparing the leather.

Brewing

Until about 1400 ale was drunk by everyone other than the very rich who could afford to drink wine mixed with water. Ale was brewed from a mixture of malt, yeast and water. The malt was prepared by allowing moistened barley to germinate at a carefully controlled temperature for several days. Then the rootlets were screened off by means of a sieve and the malt dried in a kiln before being ground in a mill. The malt was mixed with water and yeast was added to ferment the liquid. After 1400 the custom, introduced from Holland, of adding hops to the malt mixture, before fermentation took place, was adopted. The resulting liquid, beer, could be kept for a much longer time, with obvious advantages.

In Hornsea the first indication of a brewery comes in 1625 in the Manor Court Rolls regarding, "... a parcell of a cott in Southgate commonly called a kilne," which is referred to again in 1659 as a, " ... kilne lying at Marr side on the south side of the lane." It may have been outside the alehouse using this kiln that Parliamentarian soldiers traditionally broached the casks of ale in the incident at the time of the Civil War mentioned in Bedell. By 1708 this small place had been enlarged to, "... one cottage one kilne, one milne and one stable." There was also a malt kiln in Eastgate around 1677, which in 1795 is further identified as, "... a malt kiln with two cottages and a half with pasture on the North of the said cottages adjoining the pasture called Leys." In 1719 there is an entry referring to two cottages in Southgate at the corner of Football Green in which, "... the one cottage converted into a kilne and reserving the Pigeons chamber with the benefit of the Pigeons and free Liberty of egress through the kilne chamber aforesaid," seems to describe a somewhat unsanitary arrangement.

Until the end of the 18th century the sale of beer and ale to the public would have been from the bar parlours of ale houses not much bigger than the average cottage. The growth of the popularity of sea bathing for the gentry in the last half of the 18th century would see a demand for better accommodation than had been necessary for the country folk and farmers on market days. The first inn seems to have been the Old Hotel, formerly Low Hall, the property of the Acklams. This was sold by them in 1777 and became an inn and remained so until 1885 when it became a livery stables. The New Inn in the Market Place was probably opened towards the end of the 18th Century. Certainly it was flourishing in 1806 according to the poem printed in that year and given elsewhere in this book. The 1821 East Riding Directory has four inns listed in Hornsea, the other two being The Hare and Hounds which was probably in Southgate, and The Prince of Wales in the Market Place. This inn was renamed The Victoria in 1837.

Roperies or Rope Walks

The fibre which comes from the inner bark of the stem of the hemp plant, (*cannabis sativa,*) was used at one time for making a coarse cloth used by the poor for sheets and underwear, etc. However, by the 17th century hemp was grown mainly for the making of ropes and twine, for shoe and harness thread and for sacking. The expansion of overseas trade between England and the colonies in the 18th century and the consequent need for ships led to an increased demand for ropes of all sizes for the rigging of ships. Towards the end of the 18th century a bounty of 3d a stone for hemp was paid to the growers and the increased demand for rope led to the development of many rope walks in towns and villages. The hemp plant, (a member of the nettle family,) grows between three and six feet tall. After cutting, the stalks were left to "rett," (become seasoned by the weather.) They were then crushed and the fibres removed. The fibres were cleaned by a hackling board which was studded with steel nails 5 inches long. A handful of hemp was taken up, sprinkled with linseed oil, and then drawn through the pins on the board repeatedly until all the fibres were parallel. They were then laid aside in heaps for spinning.

In rope making the hemp was laid round the waist of the spinner with the ends at the back. Then some fibres were drawn out between finger and thumb and attached to one of four hooks on a large spinning wheel about 3 feet in diameter. This wheel was turned by handle, usually by a boy, at a regular pace and the spinner walked backwards down the ropewalk drawing out more fibres as he walked. When the yarn was long enough the boy detached the end from the hooks and wound it onto a winding reel which was turned with the spinner holding the end of the yarn tight. This yarn could be woven into varying thickness of rope by means of a sledge with revolving hooks which was driven down the ropewalk, twisting the yarn all the time, until a long enough length was obtained.

The Hornsea tithes of 1422 awarded to the Vicar included hemp, which presumably was used then for weaving coarse sheets, for clothing and the backing for harness. In 1746 a Thomas Byass ropemaker bought a cottage in Newbegin. He died in 1778 and his son, Robert, surrendered the copyhold cottage in Newbegin to Mr. Whytehead, Vicar of Atwick, "... to be occupied by some poor person or persons belonging to the parish of Hornsea, rent free." Robert Byass moved to 41 Southgate and had his ropewalk at the back of the house alongside the roadway to the Mere. The Byass family were still making ropes and twine there in 1840 according to the East Riding Directory of that year.

Brick Making

Although the Romans had made bricks in England the tradition disappeared during the Dark Ages until in the 13th century it was reintroduced into East Anglia from Holland. Hull and Beverley had very important brick works, Holy Trinity Church, Hull being one of the earliest large brick buildings of the 14th century to be built in England.

The earliest bricks were made by treading the wet clay with bare feet on hard ground which was strewn with hay or straw to prevent sticking. All the pebbles had to be removed from the clay because on heating these would split the brick. The clay was cut into convenient sizes, laid out to dry, and then heated in a kiln. As wood was used for fuel, the earliest bricks were thinner than the modern brick to allow the heat to penetrate. With the use of coal for fuel, the bricks could be made thicker. By the 18th century the clay was prepared in a pug mill. The coarse clay mixture was fed into a hopper and a central vertical shaft with revolving horizontal blades worked the mixture into a smooth dough. A horse or donkey was harnessed to the shaft to turn it. Any suitable patch of clay could be dug in the fields about the town. The dough was pressed into wooden moulds and left to dry for a fortnight. The bricks were taken out of the moulds and loaded into a kiln and fired for about 48 hours.

In Hornsea, according to the Manor Court Rolls, there were three bricklayers living in the town in 1700. The first mention of a brickyard in the Rolls comes in 1710 with the sale of a brickyard in Westgate. This brickyard was still in production in 1794 when it was sold to a James Bedell. It is possible that the site now called The Dell marks the position of this brickyard, since in nearly 100 years a large quantity of clay would be excavated.

Perhaps the Old Hall in the Market Place was the first brick building in Hornsea and the bricks might have been produced in the Westgate brickyard, for the alternative of transporting bricks from Beverley or Hull would have been both expensive and, in view of the demolition of the pier at Hornsea Beck, difficult. Other materials used in building, sand and lime, were produced locally. The first from "Sanpit Daile" in the East Field, and the second from burning the boulders of limestone found on the beach.

Weaving

Up to the time of the enclosures most cottages had a wool wheel or spinning wheel as part of their domestic equipment. The wool was first carded to remove soil and dirt from the fleece. This was originally done by means of teazles or thistles, (*carduus,*) but later a board set with rows of wire teeth was used. The wool was spun on the spinning wheel, then washed and dyed using dyes obtained from plants such as elder, dandelion, gorse, ragwort, etc. The fibre from flax, (called "line,") was similarly spun and dyed locally, and both wool and line would be taken to the village weaver to be woven into cloth. The weavers used simple wooden looms. The warp threads were fastened to heddle frames which were operated by a treadle, whilst the shuttle with the weft thread was passed through by hand.

In the late 17th century in Hornsea there was a weaver called John Burn who was the ancestor of the family who lived in the house which is now Hornsea Museum. The Quaker, Robert Lambert, was a weaver and lived in Southgate in the 1780's As late as 1850 Hornsea still had one weaver according to an East Riding Directory. In 1745 there was a dyer called Christopher Bainton occupying a shop in the Market Place and the list of tithes written around 1764 includes "saggarum" which is the dialect name for ragwort. The flower of this plant gave an orange dye; perhaps this was a favourite colour of the time. Other colours were obtained from gorse which gave a green dye, foxglove gave red, dandelion gave magenta, and elder gave light brown.

The Blacksmith

One of the two essential services needed in every town was that of blacksmith and most places the size of Hornsea had two smiths. However up to the end of the 18th century Hornsea seems to have had only one, and the smithy was situated at the corner of Southgate and Newbegin. In 1680 the blacksmith, a Jonathan Ilyott described his premises in the Manor Court Rolls as being. "... a cottage in Southgate being the shop joyning upon Market Place now with the kitching and the black smith shoppe joyning there to and part of the yard from the shoppe and to the west side of the little gate." However, with the increase in carriages in the town in the bathing season by the beginning of the 19th century there were two blacksmiths in the Market Place. One was at 14 and the other at 35.

Milling

The second essential service was provided by the miller. The first mills built by the Romans were water mills. The windmill seems to have been first recorded in 1320. These first windmills were post mills in which the mill stones and the shaft for the sails at the top were housed in a rectangular wooden structure which was balanced on a vertical pole with a long tail pole attached. The tail pole was used to move the whole structure of the mill around to face the wind. In the 16th century the horse mill was developed; this had the horse attached by a pole to a vertical shaft which was turned by the horse walking round a circular track. The horse mill was often built against a barn with access from the inside of the barn. From the 18th century onwards the windmills were tower mills built of brick; the sails were fixed on to a cap at the top of the mill and the driving shaft was housed in the cap. The cap could be revolved to make the sails face the wind. In all these mills the grain was fed by a hopper to be ground between two horizontal stones.

In Hornsea there is no mention of a mill in the Domesday Book; the nearest mills were at Rise and Catwick, but a mill must have been built soon after Domesday since nearly every manor came to have its own mill and Hornsea, on the evidence of the market day granted in 1257, was a thriving place. The mills were a valuable perquisite for the Lord of the Manor since all the corn grown on the manor had to be ground in the manorial mill and a toll of 1/16th could be taken from it. The first evidence of these mills is contained in the Certificate of Wind and Water Mills belonging to King James I, compiled by Sir William Spencer in 1608. In the certificate the name of the former owner of the mill is given in brackets followed by details of the tenant, etc.,

(Monastery of the Blessed Mary near the walls of the city of York)
2 windmills in Hornsey in tenancy of Richd Walker £4.0.0.
2 mills called Fosse mills near York £7.0.0.

These Hornsea mills were obviously taken over with the Manor of Hornsea by the Crown; they would have been post mills. The Manor Court Rolls refers to these two mills, when in 1659, "... a cottage in Southgate at the beck side and near to the milne house," was surrendered. A second mill is referred to in an entry in 1668, "... lying in the Cristill in Hornsey East Field near the beck milne." The area known then as Cristill has been commemorated by the Chrystal Estate and the site of this mill is identified on the earliest 6 inches to the mile Ordnance Survey map of about 1850, which marks Mill Hill, as being east of the present Cliff Road on the site of Elim Lodge. It was this mill which was "oversett" by a hurricane in 1732.

There was also a windmill in Hornsea Burton; this is shown on a map of 1663 as a post mill, and is referred to in a court action in 1584 when the ownership of, "... two tofts and a windmill in Hornsey Burton," was disputed. The site of this mill is marked on the map of 1850 and of course the present Mill Lane led to it.

As well as the two windmills in Hornsea there was a horse mill. This was situated in Eastgate, and it is mentioned in 1670 in the Manor Court Rolls as, "... the close next to George Robinson and one stable joyning upon the horse milne." Further details of the mill are given in 1671. "William Wallis leaves one horse milne and a barne and a garth called the kilne garth to his son William on condition Anne his wife shall have half the profit from said milne." It was customary to crush the malt, before brewing, in a horse mill and the reference to the kilne garth seems to show that brewing was done nearby. Taking the number of buildings in these entries, namely a millhouse, a horse mill, a barn and stable, and looking at the 1850 map, there is a group of buildings on the north side of Eastgate which might be the site of the horse mill. This would be at the northern corner of The Rise where there is still a stretch of cobble wall to be found.

Finally, around the end of the 18th century, roller mills were introduced. These were used mainly for rolling oats, and it may have been one of these that is spoken of in an entry in the Rolls in 1800, "... a messuage in Southgate with barn, stable, malt kilne and oat meal mill." A tower mill, with a brick base, was built on the Atwick Rood certainly by 1785 and possibly before. This mill continued in use until around 1900. The brick base, now converted into part of a house, still remains.

Building with Cobbles

The use of boulder stones collected from deposits of boulder clay was widespread in Holderness and examples can still be found of buildings and walls of this material all the way down the coast and for some miles inland. Lacking natural stone to quarry, this was the only material available for buildings, other than clay plastered over a wooden framework. Although the use of boulders was begun before the 13th Century, mud walled buildings, perhaps because of the ease of construction, were still common as late as the 18th Century. Poulson says that in Ulrome the Curate's house had mud walls and a thatched roof until 1782 and in 1840, speaking of that village, he says:-

> *"A short distance from the church are the Poor houses composed of mud and thatch, in front of them is an unusually large piece of water used as the Village horsepond."*

37

However, building with boulders or cobbles as they are known locally, must certainly have been extensively practised by the mid-14th century to enable such a large building as the church to be undertaken.

The source of the cobbles was the beach and in particular Atwick Gap. As late as 1920 donkeys were used to bring the stones from there. The cobbles were carried in panniers slung either side of the back of a donkey or horse. Joseph Lambert, the Quaker weaver, writing in 1801, says:-

> *"There are several of our poor neighbours who keep asses upon the back of which they hang a sort of panier into which they gather stones when the tide is out the greater part of the year for paving, building and for lime in great quantities."*

The panniers would have been woven from willow from the Mere. The first mention of a "panier man" is in 1609 at the inquisition into the loss of the Hornsea Beck pier. The last cobble building erected in Hornsea was the Infants' School built in Westgate in 1845 by Mary, Lady Strickland of Wassand. This was in use until 1935 and is now converted into a house.

The Constable family of Burton Constable, as hereditary Seigniors of Holderness were entitled to a tithe of all goods on the seashore south of Hornsea Beck. This was a right handed down from the contest of 1228. In 1862 a writ was issued by Sir Clifford Constable against John Monkman, "... to restrain from taking away gravel, sand, stones, cobbles, ballast, sea weed, shingle between High and Low Mark adjoining Hornsea Burton." Licences were issued by Sir Clifford to various people to allow them to collect building material from the beach.

The charges were:-

For every ton of stone or cobbles	three pence
For every ton of gravel	two pence
For every ton of sand	two pence

The people who took the gravel and sand were known as "cadgers."

The right to anything on the seashore North of the Beck belonged to the Lord of the Manor of Hornsea and this right is mentioned in a letter of 1810, as follows. "George Wade, Parish Clerk of Hornsea gives evidence that Joseph Wilson takes wreck for Wm. Bethell from the Meer to Atwick. He also takes groundage of all vessels which lay on. Has done so 40 years or more." The taking away of sand and stones from the seashore was banned by the Board of Trade in 1869.

Shops

In the 17th Century there were six shops in Hornsea according to the Manor Court Records. Apart from the blacksmith's shop, there would probably be a saddler's shop amongst them. The burial register shows that there was also a grocer, a milliner and a barber in Hornsea at that time.

One interesting relic of the times is a token issued in Hornsea in 1670 to be used instead of small change which was in very short supply at the time. The first tokens were issued in 1648 and they were made illegal in 1672. This token, the size of a halfpenny, shows a ship in full sail on the obverse with the words "FRANCIS RHODES" around the rim. On the reverse are the words, "IN HORNSEA 1670 HIS HALF PENNY." Timothy Rhodes, Vicar, had bought a shop in Newbegin from Thomas

The Unique Hornsea Trading Token of 1670

This late 17th century house in Southgate was lived in for many years by the Byass family who were rope makers.

39

7 The Parish

At the end of the 16th century, in the reign of Elizabeth I, a most important decision was taken by the central government for the relief of the poor of the country. Instead of relying on the hazards of individual acts of charity, the need for a compulsory poor rate was accepted. By this means the large proportion of the population which was at that time poor and destitute would be relieved. This was in effect the first step towards a welfare state and because the Poor Relief, as it was called, was to be administered by officers appointed by the parish, it was also the beginning of local government.

With the increase in the importance of the parish came a corresponding decrease in the importance of the manor and the Manor Court. For instance, the Constable, once chosen by the court was to be henceforth an officer of the parish, chosen by the Justices of the Peace. Also chosen by the Justices of the Peace were the two or more Overseers of the Poor who were responsible for levying the Poor Rate throughout the parish. Each parish had to accept responsibility for everyone born in that parish who became destitute, and the law was that the poor should be returned to that parish from wherever else they may have settled.

The other officers of the parish, the Churchwardens and Surveyor of the Highways were elected every Easter by the parishioners from the leading yeomen of the parish. In some towns and villages in Holderness part of the Churchwardens' accounts and the Constables' accounts have survived. In Hornsea, however, there are very few parish documents extant and consequently only a broad outline of the parish organization can be given.

Looking at the work undertaken by the officers in more detail, the **Constables** of the parish, usually two in number, had to give money and lodging to poor travellers on their way home to their own parishes. They were also responsible for keeping the peace and raising the alarm after a robbery or an assault. When taxes were levied on the number of servants in a household and the number of windows in a house, it was the duty of the Constable to assess the householders for these taxes. In the Hornsea Manor Court Rolls at various times in the 17th and 18th centuries the election of the two parish constables is recorded, and there is one reference to the taxes in this entry. "Elizabeth Watkinson has house, kitching, and stables in Newbegin and Southgate for three years from Lady Day 1736 paying half of the taxes except window money and to pay to Rebecca Weatherill one shilling a year."

The **Overseers of the Poor** had not only the duty of levying the poor rate throughout the parish. They also had to help provide apprenticeships for poor children so that they might be trained for a useful occupation. In Hornsea details of two examples of the work of the Overseers of the Poor have been preserved in two entries in the Manor Court Rolls. The first in 1719 says:-

> *"Jane the wife of John Midforth the sol^d died leaving three daughters two of them being born durng his absence and the law not making them bastards, he the said John Midforth Coming home upon furloe at the news of his wifes death, and sold a parcel of a cottage which he had in Westgate and did agree with the overseers and other the inhabitants of Hornsey for five pounds to them in hand paid by ye sd John Midforth to be for ever quitt of and from all manner of Charges and Incumbrances concerning the Education and Bringing up of any of ye Daughters aforesd in Witness thereof we hear sett our hands (Signed by the Jury of 12.)"*

The settlement of only £5 on the two girls is in contrast to the amount thought necessary for the boy who is the subject of the second entry in the Manor Rolls in 1735:-

> *"William Robson bound unto 6 Church wardens and overseers of the poore of Bridlington in the penal sum of £100 condition for maintaining and keeping Ralph Craven a male Bastard child and for indemnifying the said Township of Bridlington."*

The **Surveyor of Highways** was responsible for deciding how many days of labour each household should supply to making up the roads, and which horses and carts should carry the stones and gravel used for repairing the roads. The people of the parish were supposed to be responsible for the upkeep of all the roads in that parish, but it seems that rich and poor alike regarded this as labour lost. As one writer put it, "... the rich do so cancel their portion and the poor so loiter in their labours that of all the six scarcely two days work are performed." The roads in Holderness were generally regarded as impassable in the winter months. Even as late as 1786 the roads marked on a map of that date are only marked with a dotted line. In the year 1688 the election of two Surveyors of the Highways in Hornsea is recorded in the Manor Court Rolls.

There were four **Churchwardens** instead of the usual two for the parish of Hornsea which included not only the town of Hornsea, but also Hornsea Beck, Hornsea Burton, and Long Riston. The Churchwardens had several duties to perform in the parish. First, they

41

were responsible for the care and upkeep of the fabric of the church other than the chancel which was the responsibility of the impropiator of the Rectorial tithes. In 1575 the Churchwardens complained about the state of the chancel of the church and their complaint is recorded in the records of the Holderness Deanery:-

> *"Horneseye Their Chauncel is out of reparatyon and bath continewed the space of ten yeres in defalt of John Armitage who out to repaire the same."*

The Churchwardens were also to be scrutineers of the moral life of the parish and again in the Holderness Deanery records is an example of their judgement. "In Hornseye four fornicators." At the same time in nearby Withernsea there were, it seems, eight "fornicators." A third duty was that of collecting money from charitable people in the parish for the relief of victims of natural disasters, such as fire or flood, which occurred throughout the country. The victim of the disaster obtained a written authorisation, or "brief" as it was called, from the local Justices of the Peace and took it from parish to parish.

The only record of payment on "briefs" in Hornsea are those written on the back page of the Register of Births, Marriages and Deaths for the years 1654 to 1695. This reads:-

> *"Gathered for the inhabitants of Stillingfleet in ye parish of H.ornsea inᶜ Long Riston April 9th 1665 the sum of three shillings threepence*
>
> *Gathered for Henry Lister of Gisborough in the parish of Hornsea inᶜ Long Riston May 28th 1665 the sum of five shillings threepence*
>
> *Gathered for Nathan Hoyle Sept 2nd 1666 2.8d of William Twinning Collector*
>
> *Gathered upon a Brief for Melcombe Regis in the County of Dorset July 11th 1667 The sum of one shilling and elevenpence"*

When the freak hurricane struck Hornsea in 1732 a "brief" was obtained from the magistrates in Beverley to help towards raising the £250 needed to repair the damage.

Details of the Parish from the Church registers, etc.

From the register of births it seems that the favourite Christian names for boys were George, John and William with a surprising number of Marmadukes, possibly in imitation of the Constable family, and a solitary "Lancoloot." The girls were usually Anne, Jane, Sarah, Elizabeth or Mary, but in 1685 there was a Theodosia and a Naamah.

The houses in the town up to the early 17th century were usually built with mud walls, but by the end of that century these were being replaced by cobble walls. These early cobble cottages had a central massive chimneystack and examples of these early cobble cottages are to be found in Southgate. In those days the main living room was usually called the hall or the fire house. The parlour was the name usually given to the bedroom, although the parlour was often used as a store for household utensils as well. The kitchen was always called, "the kitching," and the cottages were often of one storey and always, of course, with thatched roofs.

In the Manor Court Rolls the number of rooms of a cottage is sometimes given, as in 1635 when a cottage in Southgate is defined as, "being the hall house, parlour and kitching." In some cases the cottages were divided on the death of the owner amongst the heirs as in another cottage in Southgate which is defined as, "... the two parlours and one chamber being the northend of the said house and one littill coale House in the back yard." In some instances the jury of the Manor Court had to arbitrate between rival claimants as in 1653 on the death of a cottager:-

> "Mary Hall and Ellis Dutch is her daughter and next heares betwixt them as followeth: Mary is heire to the Hall house and parler next the Street and a little house joining on the backe side, after the death of Ann Roundfatt with egress. and regress on the backe side called the garth. Ellis Dutch is heire to two low parlers and a little meale house joining on them and the milne haues and egresse and regresse on the garth, this being according to a division made betwixt them."

There are many entries defining the right of way, or egress and regress, as it was called; it may be that newly built cobbled wall boundaries were making it necessary to define rights of way more clearly. The description of the vicarage given in the Terrier of 1764 shows the variety of building materials in use in Hornsea by the 18th century:-

> "The Vicarage House is 20 yards long and 6 broad built chiefly with brick and covered with Tyles. The kitchen, four low Rooms which are floored with Brick except the Dining Room which is floored with Wood, four chambers besides Garretts. There is a large yard in which is a Barn and stable covered with Thatch, an Orchard fenced

with a Clay wall. The Churchyard is fenced towards South with a Stone wall covered with Brick. There are 6 or 7 sycamore trees growing in Church yard valued at 5 shillings."

This vicarage had been unroofed in the hurricane of 1732 and was the building standing on Newbegin which was pulled down when the present Vicarage, standing back from the road, was built in 1831. Only the trees in the churchyard and the cobble boundary wall remain today.

Details of the household furnishings of a typical pre-Enclosure cottage can be found in an Inventory of the goods and effects of George Hornby of Hornsea, Husbandman, dated October 30th 1728. This member of the Hornby family lived at the cottage now 36 Southgate which figures in the entry for 1670 quoted in the previous chapter:-

	£	s	d
Imprimis¹ his purse and apparel	7	0	0
It.² In the firehouse³ A dresser with eight dishes of Pewter and nine plates, some brass implements a fir table with frame,			
Four chairs, a little Iron Range an iron Pott with other implements	3	6	8
It. In the Kitchinge and Milke house a Table A Milk Tub a Churn,			
Some bowls, with other Impements		13	4
It. In the Chamber⁴ A bed with bedding a kneading tubb, two			
Wheeles⁵ some wooll with other implts		15	6
It. Two draught beasts, three Cows, two stears⁶ two whyes⁷ two			
half gate stears⁸ and two calfes	37	10	0
It. Two draught horses, a Mare and fole five years old and a Colt			
three years old	15	0	0
It. Corn in the Barn and Stack thrash'd and to thrash and Wheat,			
Beanes and Oates	26	0	0
It. Wheat Sowne Downe	15	10	0
It. One Waine⁹ and waine geare, plough and plough geare with			
foure Harrows and other impts of husbandry	5	5	0
It. A Pigg and some Poultry	1	0	0
It. Some hay in stack	2	10	0
It. Forgotten goods		3	4
	116	8	4

NOTES: 1 *Imprimis* - First 2 *It. (Item)* - Also 3 *firehouse* - living room 4 *chamber* - bedroom 5 *wheele* - spinning wheel 6 *stear* - mature bull or ox 7 *whye* - heifer 8 *half gate stear* - young animal, counted as only half a "gate" when put out to pasture 9 *waine* - large two wheeled cart

It seems from this inventory, according to the entry of the two "draught beasts" listed with the cows, that ploughing was still done by oxen.

The cottage living room with the dresser displaying the pewter dishes and the brass saucepans and candlesticks is easily visualised, with the fire burning most days of the year. The bare simplicity of the furniture has no carpets or curtains to soften the effect. The self sufficiency of the cottage way of life meant a busy time for the housewife, who must churn the butter, bake the bread, feed the pigs and poultry, as well as spin her own wool and flax which the village weaver would later make into cloth.

Late 17th century cobble cottages in Southgate

Sunset and Corner Cottages, Back Westgate. Originally one dwelling, the presence of a cruck blade in the roof suggests an early date, although most of the present building is early 18th century.

8 The Quakers in Hornsea

In 1651 George Fox, the founder of the Society of Friends, visited Holderness, a visit which led to the formation of several Meetings of Friends in villages throughout the area. Records show that by 1660 groups of Friends were to be found in Sigglesthorne, Ulrome, Owstwick, Patrington, Withernsea, Paull and Hornsea. The name "Quakers" was first given to the movement in 1656 by Justice Bennet of Derby, "... who," said George Fox, "called us Quakers because we bid them tremble at the word of God." The name persisted until the end of the 18th century when the name "The Society of Friends" came into use. Quakers had always addressed as "Friend" anyone either inside their Society or without.

George Fox had become disillusioned with the actions of many professed Christians and set out to form a religious society according to the pattern of the New Testament. From this point of view there was no need of a special building in which to hold services, and indeed Fox always referred slightingly to churches as "steeple houses" to emphasize his lack of reverence towards them. Nor was there any need for an ordained ministry since all believers were thought of as being in the priesthood. In the simplicity of the New Testament there was no need for ceremony between fellow humans and therefore no need for "hat honour" as the Quakers called it, nor was there need for the taking of oaths. These beliefs of the Quakers led them to refuse to pay tithes, which went to support the clergy, or to take oaths when giving evidence. It also led them to interrupt at services in church and as early as 1655 a proclamation of Cromwell had noted their "...rude and un-Christian disturbance of ministers."

In Hornsea, the first instance of a Quaker being punished for his beliefs is in 1656 when Oliver Ketteridge of Hornsea Burton was fined for refusing to take an oath. He also suffered 13 weeks' imprisonment in 1659 for refusing to pay the parish clerk's wage and he received another prison sentence in January 1660 on being taken at a meeting at Sigglesthorne. An example of the punitive treatment of the Quakers at that time comes from the village of Tunstall where John Spencer, on refusing to pay tithes of 14d, had a cow, valued at £3 10s, taken from him to be sold to pay the tithes.

The year 1660 saw a short sharp campaign by the authorities against the Quakers in Yorkshire, when 535 were imprisoned in December for refusing to take the Oath of Allegiance to the recently restored King Charles II. Most of them were released, however, in the following February although some were not so fortunate. Two Quakers from Ulrome, George Hartas and William Stang, were imprisoned in York Castle where George Hartas caught the jail fever and died. Soon after his death, his widow, also a Quaker, was taken out of her sick bed and taken away to prison, leaving behind her ten fatherless children.

Amongst those taken in 1660 was Peter Acklam, a member of the most important Quaker family in Hornsea. He was:-

"... sent for from his own house by John Bellasis, Governor of Hull, who without cause committed him to the Custody of a Marshall. After two weeks confinement he was had before several Justices who tendered him the Oath of Allegiance and for refusing to swear Committed him to York Castle."

In a record of York Castle prisoners of this time are the names, Major Acklam and John Starr, said to be, *"... dangerous obstinate and quaking speakers."* Both Peter Acklam of Hornsea and George Hartas of Ulrome were men of substance. George Hartas was Lord of the Manor of Ulrome and Peter Acklam's son was to become Lord of the Manor of Hornsea in 1684.

The Acklams of Hornsea were members of an important Holderness family who originally came from Dringhoe and Skipsea. These Acklams were not the first family of that name in Hornsea as there are records from 1629 of a "Goo Arklom" (George Acklam.) This George Acklam had the manor of Bewholme and, as a Royalist sympathiser, was fined heavily under the Commonwealth with fines of nearly £800 being exacted in 1653. The Dringhoe Acklams on the other hand were Parliamentarian sympathisers. Peter Acklam I served as a major under Colonel Hugh Bethell of Rise at the Second Siege of Scarborough in 1648. When the castle surrendered, Acklam took the news to London and was awarded £40 by Parliament.

Thomas Acklam of Dringhoe bought from Nicholas Moore in 1653 two cottages in Westgate, a Garner (a barn) and a cottage called West Close. In 1658 and 1659 he was an Affeeror and given the title "gentleman" in the Manor Court Rolls. It is possible that Thomas did not become a Quaker until after 1660 since he would have had to swear allegiance to become a member of the court jury. In 1661 Timothy Rhodes bought a cottage in Southgate from Thomas Acklam and in November 1664 the same Timothy Rhodes, now Vicar of Hornsea, bought a shop in Newbegin from him. Three months later in February 1665 an Information was laid against Thomas's son, Peter, by this Timothy Rhodes describing Peter Acklam as, *"... the chiefe of the sectaries in the East Riding,"* an interesting sequence of events.

In the Information it was said:-

47

*" ... that on Friday the 10th February between 11 and 12 o'clock
he saw go into the house of Peter Acklam of Hornsea, Pursewell
Musom, John Raines junr, Oliver Kitwige (sic) and his wife all of
Hornsea and Robert Lampley of Bridlington and divers other
persons unknown to this informer to the number as he conceives of
or about one hundred most of which persons he conceives came out
about two hours and a half later. And further saith that the said
Peter Acklam has had formerly several other meetings frequently in
his house since his last releasement from his imprisonment att Hull
upon Sundays and other days."*

To the charge laid against him, Peter Acklam made a rather
evasive reply:-

*"Friend seeing there is nothing testified against me of any breach of
law but that some men and women were seen going towards and
coming from my house which is insufficient, to make me guilty of
transgressing that law which is made as a snare to enthrall us and
by your examination of me that what I have been informed is all you
have against me. In love to thee I admonish thee not to do so unjust
an Act as to send me to prison for the same, seeing it is contrary to
thy oath as thou art a justice of peace to do anything that is unjust.
This only signify thee as thou art the chief magistrate in the county
and hath the powers thereof in thy hand so I leave it to thy
consideration not to trouble thee with more at present."*

The reference to the chief magistrate in the county may have
meant one of the Constable family of Burton Constable. Certainly it was
Nicholas Constable who committed him for trial in 1678, prosecuted
under the terms of the Statute of Absence from National Worship. That
Nicholas Constable was, "... a person much inclinable to Popery," was
remarked by the Quakers of the time who found it ironic that a Catholic
should be helping to imprison Peter Acklam, since the Catholics could
also be penalised under the same statute.

The pattern of fines and imprisonments did not deter the
Quakers from living their lives according to their beliefs, as a separate
people apart from the community around them. Marriage to people
outside the Society was not allowed. For instance, a member of the
Owstwick Meeting, Margaret Rayne, was admonished for courting a man
not of the Quaker faith and testified, "Since I gave way to the enemy of
my soul's peace I have not prospered in my outward condition and
darkness and dread have been upon my inward soul. I now pray and

plead that ye 'Lords people' should pray for me, so that the Inward Light should come to me."

The harassment of the Quakers finally ceased with the Act of Toleration of 1682 and two years later, in 1684, Peter Acklam II became Lord of the Manor of Hornsea. The family had prospered steadily throughout the previous thirty years in spite of the fines and imprisonments. As well as the property in Westgate already mentioned, the Rectory House, which stood on freehold land to the north of the Church, had been bought, probably at the same time, and it may have been this building which held the 100 people in the Information of 1665. Bedell said that the Old Rectory was pulled down in the reign of James II, which was from 1685 to 1688.

In January 1665 Thomas Acklam bought a cottage called Low Close in Southgate from John Newsom and Elinor his wife, and on his death in the summer of 1667, was buried in the garden of this cottage, as was his wife, Anna Maria, who also died that year. As Quakers they did not accept the need to be buried in consecrated ground. Thomas left all his property, including four shops in Newbegin, to his son Peter and it was Peter Acklam who enlarged the cottage at Low Close to three cottages between May and November 1675. This property sometimes called Low Hall was let to George Atkinson with the stipulation:-

"...that the new garden plot be returned to the use of the said Peter Acklam and Alice his wife, Peter Acklam and Thomas Acklam his sons and Anna Maria his daughter for a burying plot when and as often as they or any of them shall desire the same."

In 1691 the Vicar recorded in the parish register, "Feb 1st Mr. Peter Acklom buried in his garden." There were finally nine Acklams buried in the garden of Low Hall, the last one in 1760 being Peter Acklam III, grandson of the builder of Low Hall and some of the gravestones are still in the garden of the house. There was a gravestone of this period used as a doorstep at 41 Southgate and on the rebuilding of this cottage this was incorporated into the garden terrace.

The second Peter Acklam, who became Lord of the Manor of Hornsea in 1684, built the Old Hall. Market Place sometime between 1685 and 1688. On his death in 1744 he left £20 to the poor of Hornsea and £30 to the poor of Owstwick Monthly Meeting. As his only child, a girl, had died in 1700, his property passed to his nephew Peter. When this Peter in his turn died in 1760, he left property with a rent of 20shillings a year to the Overseers of the Poor to buy gowns for poor women. To the remaining Quakers in Hornsea he left a meeting place in Westgate subsequently called Quaker Cottage. Details of this meeting place are given in the Hornsea entry in the Archbishop Herring's Visitation to the Diocese of York in 1743:-

"There are 133 families in ye Parish 4 of which are Dissenters one Popish family, two of the sect of Quaker and the fourth Presbyterian. We have no Meeting House but one for Quakers. They meet twice a week on Sundays and Thursdays there are seldom more than 4 or 5 go to the meeting, no Teachers amongst them."

Another reference to the Meeting House comes in the Manor Court Rolls in 1750. "A barn or garth adjoining upon Bitchis Lane being one Cottage, a Garnor or Meeting house with a staboll." In 1760 on his death, it is entered as follows:-

"Peter Acklam did hereby give a cottage in Westgate in Hornsea formerly a parcell of a cottage near adjoyning being occupied as a stable with ye yard and belonging to John Storr and Isaac Smith Both of Owstwick in Holderness and to Robert Milner of Kingston upon Hull their heirs and assignes in Special Trust and Confidence that they shall stand seized and possessed thereof to the Sole Use and benefit of the People called Quakers forever and that the said premises or a part thereof shall be constantly maintained in due repair for performance of Publick Worship by any of the said people so long as may be found Expedient and if the same be found of no use then the Trustees to sell the same and apply the produce thereof for the sole use and Benefit of the people called Quakers belonging Owstwick Monthly Meeting forever."

The Acklams left Hornsea, selling Low Hall which subsequently became an inn, in 1777, and the Old Hall passed in 1821 to the Constable family of Wassand.

Another indication of the number of Quakers in Hornsea in this period is to be found at the front of the Register of Burials in an undated memorandum:-

131 Families in this Parish
297 Communicants
No papists, no dissenters except 3 Quakers

From entries in the Manor Court Rolls it is possible to identify the other two Quaker families. In April 1782 under the list of sworn tenants is the entry, "Tenant Robert Lambert being a Quaker affirmed." Again, in 1785, a widow, Ann Watson, affirms instead of being sworn in as a tenant. Robert Lambert, despite his Quakerism, was one of the four churchwardens at the time of the diocesan visitation in 1743. It is probable that he was a tied churchwarden who had to take his turn in the office by virtue of being the tenant of a certain house or piece of land. George Prudhom, another of the churchwardens at the time of the visitation, challenged the legality of the Acklams' ownership of their Hornsea property. This attempt took place at the Manor Court of October 1781, when George Prudhom presented a writ, "...seising the tenements and appurtenances sur diseissin en le posh," as the clerk of the court puts it. This attempt quite rightly failed. However, the list of property involved shows how much the Acklams had prospered since 1653, some thirty cottages and 200 acres of land being accredited to them.

The Quakers continued in Hornsea after the Acklams left. In 1785 comes an entry in the Rolls referring to the cottage in Westgate and, "... the yard now used as a Burying ground for the said people called Quakers." Robert Lambert died in 1791 and his son, Joseph, became one of the trustees of the Meeting House.

It has been said that the Quakers were, on the whole, better educated than the average person of the day and certainly they were very industrious. Joseph Lambert seems to have been a case in point. He was a weaver and also had his small holdings of land in the Hornsea fields. In 1801 and 1803 he was listed in the Hommage of the Manor Court. At the foot of the entries for 1802 is written, "J. Lambert, vera copia." Obviously he had been asked to look over the clerk's copy of the proceedings, which shows the esteem held by the ordinary villager for his ability. Another indication of this esteem lies in a letter written by him in March 1801 on behalf of the cottagers when the awards at the time of the enclosure of the Hornsea open fields was being calculated. In this letter, addressed to one of the arbitrators J. Dickinson, he enumerates the animals that each cottager kept and the financial benefit they received and he ends the letter, "I am very respectfully the Friend of the poor cottagers, advocate without fee or reward excepting my portion of claim." His portion of claim was in fact only a small one for, on his death in 1805, he left a cottage and garden and some six acres of land only. As a spokesman for the poorer cottagers, his education, ability and steadfastness must have been of great service to that section of the community who suffered most from the Enclosures. The death of his widow, Dinah, in 1818 saw the departure of the last of the Quakers in Hornsea for the time being.

Within the last few years a number of members of the Society of Friends have come to live in Hornsea and, after renovation, Quaker Cottage, the cottage which was the original Meeting House in Westgate, was re-opened as such in December 1972, after a lapse of over 150 years.

Quaker Gravestones at Low Hall, Southgate

Recorded by George Poulson, 1840 and now lost

■ Here lyes ALYCE, wife of PETER ACKLOME who died A.D. 1692 aged 76

■ Here lyes ANNA MARIE daughter of PETER and ALICE ACKLOM who died 19th of June 1734 age 68

■ Near this place lie the remains of ISABELLA ACKLOM, widow of PETER ACKLOM who died Dec 5th 1758 aged 92

Recorded by the East Yorkshire Family History Society, c1996

■ Here lieth the remains of PETER son of PETER and ALICE ACKLOM who died ye 29th of July 1744 aged near 85

■ Here lyes ANNA MARIA dter of P ACKLOME Junr: who dyd A.D. 1700 aged 12

■ Here lyes THOMAS son of P ACKLOME who dyd A.D. 1699 aged 38

■ Here lyes PETER son of THOMAS ACKLOME who dyed A.D. 1690 aged 72 years

■ Here lyes THOMAS & ANNA MARIA ACKLOM his wife who both dyd A.D. 1667 eached aged 72 years

← **Low Hall, Southgate**
This house was probably built by the Quaker Peter Acklam I around 1675. The land at the rear was used as a burial ground for the Acklam family between 1691 and 1760.

Quaker Cottage, →
Back Westgate
In the Manor Court Rolls. this cottage is referred to as being adjacent to a barn which was used as a meeting house.

Hornsea Charities

DAY'S RENT CHARGES

In his will, dated 14th May 1616, Mr. William Day left 40 shillings yearly charged upon his lands in Hornsea Burton to be given to the poor of Hornsea at Christmas and Easter. The lands were calculated as consisting of 21 acres of land in the parish of Hornsea, and in 1823 the Charity Commissioners reported that the rent was regularly paid to the church wardens and distributed by them. Mr. Day and his wife Thomasine had defended their possession of, "... a messuage of three cottages and lands at Hornsey, Hornsea Burton and Great Hatfield," in 1612 in an action taken by John Bedell. On William Day's death on 22nd May 1616 at the age of 34, the Vicar of Hornsea, Theophilus Chimley, composed a delightful epitaph with the typical play upon words of the period:-

> "If that man's life be likened to a day
> One here interr'd in youth did lose a day
> By death, and yet no loss to him at all,
> For he a threefold day gain'd by his fall:
> One day of rest in bliss celestial
> Two days on earth by gifts terrestryall
> Three pounds at Christmas, three at Easter Day
> Given to the poore until the world's last day.
> This was no cause to heaven; but consequent
> Who thither will, must tread the steps he went.
> For why? Faith, hope, and christian charity
> Perfect the house framed for eternity."

(Theophilus Chimley held the living from 1607 to 1631, and seems to have settled in Hornsea on his retirement. There is reference in the Manor Court Rolls to a half oxgang of land he owned at Northorp in 1640. His son, William, was a member of the "hommage" in 1665, and had in his turn a son, Theophilus. This Theophilus had as his only child, a spinster called Fortune who died in 1725.)

ACKLAM'S RENT CHARGE

On his death in 1758 Peter Acklam III charged his property, Low Hall, with the payment of 20 shillings yearly to the Overseers of the Poor every Lady Day, (March 25th.) This was to be used by them to buy sixteen yards of serge for dresses for two poor women of Hornsea. The Commissioners reported that in 1823 three poor women were being clothed by this charity.

SMITHSON'S RENT CHARGES

In 1731 a charge on land was left in Hornsea Burton by a Mr. Smithson, an Excise Officer, to yield 9 shillings a year to provide twelve threepenny loaves for the poor at Christmas, Easter and Whitsun. (The property was later owned by a Mrs. Brough.)

TOWN STOCK

In the Manor Court Rolls are several entries referring to small sums given by parishioners of Hornsea for the relief of the poor. This money was used to buy wool, flax, hemp, wood, iron and other materials in order to provide work for the poor or unemployed. These materials were known as the Town Stock. In addition, some parishioners made extra donations and by 1785 a total of £70 had been amassed, which was used by the Overseers of the Poor to pay for the building of four parish cottages for the use of paupers. (These cottages stood on the site of the Pickering Almshouses in Newbegin.)

In 1788, "Cornwell Baron Wilson, his heirs and assigns did yearly pay to Robert Croft, Vicar of Hornsea or his successors one annuity of thirty shillings payable at Christmas, Easter and Whit Sunday amongst the poor people residing within the parish."

YOUNG'S CHARITY

In 1780 Robert Byass, rope maker, surrendered a copyhold cottage in Newbegin for some poor person belonging to the parish. Four years later David Austin and his wife, Ann, left land, the rent to be used for the repair of this cottage. From the details given, it was the land once called St. Nicholas Mount now occupied by 64 to 76 Newbegin. In 1823 the land was let as a garden at a rent of 16 shillings to, "... the widow Scaife." (Mother of John Scaife, founder of the Independent Chapel.) Some years later the widow of the rector of Catwick left money to buy the cottage and land outright, and the charity then became known as Young's Charity. The cottage was finally sold in 1928.

10 Games, Sports and Customs up to the Time of the Enclosures

Up to the time of the Enclosures, the seasons of the year, the religious festivals, and the cycle of work on the land, were the occasion for a series of holidays and festivities in Hornsea. These innocent games and pastimes of a bygone pastoral age were still fondly remembered by older villagers when E.W. Bedell was collecting material for his book on Hornsea published in 1848.

The custom in Lent was to have eggs and collops to eat on Shrove Monday, as well as the traditional pancakes on Shrove Tuesday. On Ash Wednesday everyone played a game called "Tut-ball" on the Common by the Mere; the local saying being that, "Those who did not play Tut-ball on Ash Wednesday would be sick in Harvest time."

On Holy Thursday the vicar, the churchwardens and the parishioners used to beat the bounds of the parish which involved walking around the perimeter of the parish and by so doing impressing on the villagers' minds in a pre-literate age the size and shape of the parish. This activity also served to check that no boundary markers had been removed and that no new buildings had been erected and were avoiding paying the parish rate.

May Day was the day when the cattle were turned into the fresh grass on the Common. Whit week, the pleasantest time of the year, when the spring sowing was over and the hard work of the harvest still to come, had a whole series of entertainment for the village. On Whit Sunday, the seventh Sunday after Easter, two young girls went around the village collecting flowers which were made into a garland at the neatherd's house. On Whit Monday the first two milkmaids to reach the two pasture fields were called "Queens of the Pasture." All the milkmaids had dinner at the neatherd's and they were summoned to it by the two Queens and by the music of a fiddler. After the dinner the milkmaids danced until milking time. Monday's dance for the milkmaids was followed by a dance for married couples on the Wednesday and a dance on Saturday for the whole village. All these dances would be held in empty barns, cleaned and decorated for the occasion, with the music of the fiddler to dance to.

On Midsummer Eve, June 23rd, there was a bonfire, and of course the end of the harvesting was celebrated by feasting and merrymaking. November 5th had the traditional bonfire and there were also cakes and ale at Martinmas, November 11th. At Christmas the "waits" went round the village singing carols and there was "wassailing" at the New Year, an occasion for heavy drinking. Some of these customs date from early Christian times and some, the Midsummer bonfire and the Harvest feasting, date from an even earlier time.

The 17th and 18th centuries saw a great increase in interest in blood sports and field sports, and Hornsea was no exception. In the middle of the 17th century land near Northorpe changed in name from "Hopper Green" to "Cockpit." Obviously cockfighting contests were held here.

After the winter fair, held on December 17th, the afternoon was enlivened by bull baiting. A bull was tied to a stake and dogs specially bred for their fighting spirit were set on the beast and in a good day's "sport" several dogs would be killed before the bull became too weak to defend itself. The stake for tethering the bull stood in the Market Place, on the site still known as The Bullring until 1800. There is mention in 1732 in the Manor Court Rolls of a cottage being, "... near the bullring." It seems likely too, that horse racing took place on the wide stretch of sands left after the destruction of Hornsea Beck from 1750 onwards, for in that year John Greenhead, jockey, was buried in Hornsea.

In the 18th century, it seems that football matches were held between neighbouring villages although the game of football may have been played for many years previously in Hornsea. The game of football was said to have originated in Viking times when the head of a defeated enemy was used as the ball. A more convenient adjunct in later times was found to be the inflated bladder of a cow. Football Green was an area of permanent pasture as shown in the Rolls in 1626 when Bonnit Wilson, "... surrenders one ley in Footoball greene." With a stretch of permanent grassland and a plentiful supply of unwanted bladders from the tannery on the side of Hornsea Beck, it was inevitable that "Footoball" should be played on the green.

In the contests between villages the winning team was the one to get the ball back to its own village. Bedell speaks of one old man who remembered one such match played between Sigglesthorne and Hornsea. The kick-off was at a spot midway between the villages. On arriving in front of the Old Hall, Wassand the teams were given a refreshing drink of ale by Mr. Constable. The Hornsea team was the stronger and punted the ball from Wassand along the south side of the Mere into Hornsea town street. These games would finish with the enclosure of the town fields and the setting out of hedgerows.

The older men of Hornsea would have a game of bowls to entertain them. The area between Westgate and Back Westgate was in 1745 known as Booling Green or Westgate Garth according to the Rolls.

Sea fishing was not a prosperous occupation, owing to the shifting of the sea bed due to the strong currents which prevent the growth of weed. Apart from crabs, fish was brought into the village from Skipsea and other places. The fresh water fishing of the Mere was excellent, however. It was owned by the Constable family and, from time to time, could be fished on payment of a small sum to the landlord of the New Inn, (now the Pike and Heron.) The fishing and the bird life are all enthusiastically described in a poem dated 1806 and written by Edward Anderson, Master of the "*Jemima*" in the Lisbon trade. The last four lines are of interest for they describe the changes taking place in the countryside at that time.

Hornsea Mere

Many go there to fish for pleasure's sake
But they must always pay for what they take.
When caught they weigh it at the New Inn door
The money it is given to the poor.
This lake is two miles long and one mile broad
And both with fish and fowl it is well stor'd
And in the midst if it an island lies
Where sea birds breed and for miles you hear their cries.
I went there in a boat one morn in Spring
The cries around me made my ears to ring,
Thousands of birds were flying round my head,
So many nests that clear I could not tread
Without breaking their eggs, in vain to strive,
And with young birds the weeds seem'd all alive.
The old ones cry'd, "Begone," they seem'd to say
And flew close at me as I went away.
The swans so stately held their heads so high
They too did hiss me as I pass'd them by.
They flapp'd their wings and at me they did stare
And seem'd to say, "What business have you there?"
I never saw, in countries I've gone o'er
So many in so small a spot before.
Since I came home, as I this country view
The towns, the fields, now everything looks new.
The old thatch'd cottages have ta'en their flight
And new til'd houses now appear in sight.

11 Hornsea in Peril

The Spanish Armada, 1588

From the few records available it is possible to get some idea of the preparations made in the locality of Hornsea at the time of the threatened invasion of the Spanish Armada in 1588. The original plan for the subjugation of the English heretics was for the Armada to sail to Flanders and to transport the army of the Duke of Parma from there to England. The possibility of landing his Spanish army, comprising the most experienced soldiers in Europe, was a very dangerous threat to England. The flat east coast was difficult to defend and only local inexperienced militia were available to repel an invader.

The first necessity was to have a speedy warning system ready to alert the local commanders. This was provided by a network of beacons set up along the coast of Holderness. There were three beacons each at Aldbrough, Mappleton, Hornsea, Skipsea and Barmston. All of them had barrels of tar set up on high stakes. They were guarded day and night by watchmen with instructions to light the beacons in certain circumstances. If ships in the Humber or on the sea acted suspiciously one beacon was to be lit; if there were great numbers of ships which might be enemy ships they were to light two beacons; all three beacons were to be lit if the enemy landed.

These coastal beacons would give warning to two places inland - Bainton and Rudston, which in turn would light their beacons to spread the warning still further over the countryside. Another method of giving the alarm in the event of an invasion was to ring all the church bells. To avoid confusion there were to be no bells rung for any church service meanwhile.

After the alarm it was expected that all able-bodied men would take up arms against the Spanish invaders. To find what arms were available for the local defence force in Holderness one of the magistrates of the area, Sir Christopher Hildyard of Winestead, drew up a "Certificate of Generall Muster." This showed the number of fighting men in each village and the weapons they possessed. According to this certificate Hornsea had 46 able-bodied men, Seaton had 10, Sigglesthorne 12, Leven 24 and Skipsea 26. The Hornsea troop consisted of 5 pikemen, 31 billmen, 8 calevers (a type of musket) and two archers.

As well as the weapons possessed by these men, there was in the parish a stock of arms available for defence against gangs of armed robbers. Hornsea could provide one corselet, (armour to cover the body,) one bow, one sheaf of arrows, one jacke, (a coat serving the purpose of mail armour,) one skull, (a protective headgear,) one bill, (a hook ended spear,) and two murrions, (helmets without a visor.)

As well as providing armed men, each parish had to undertake to drive all the cattle, sheep and grain out of reach of the enemy. All householders had to have ready a month's supply of meal or bread to feed them as they travelled inland whilst driving their cattle away from the enemy.

Thanks to the defeat of the Armada at sea these plans were never put into action, but they were used as a guide some 200 years later when England was again threatened by invasion during the wars against France between 1793 and 1815.

During the years of the American War of Independence the Royal Navy did not have complete command of the sea around the British Isles. In 1779 John Paul Jones, the famous American sailor, was able to attack shipping almost at will along the East coast. His most daring exploit was to attack in September that year a convoy bound from the Baltic. This battle took place off Flamborough Head. During this period the Northumberland Militia was stationed at Hornsea. The story that Jones fired cannon balls at Rolston Hall is unsubtantiated.

The Wars against France 1793-1815

During these wars the threat of an invasion of the East coast of England was imminent for several years. The French troops had defeated the Austrian and Prussian armies and invaded Italy. By 1797 only the British were able to oppose the French. With complete control over the coast of France, Flanders and Holland it was obvious that urgent measures must be taken. As the military commander General Scott put it:-

> *"that the coast of Holderness which lies so immediately exposed to the Enemy should be Put into such a state of preparation for defence as under the Divine Protection may render ineffectual and finally defeat every attempt on the Part of our Inveterate Enemies and that with United Hands and Hearts we may defend and secure our Invaluable liberties and Property against all Invaders."*

A similar method of warning by beacon as the Elizabethan one was adopted. The Hornsea beacon was built on the highest point in the parish, some 74 yards from the sea, north of the road leading to the site of Hornsea Beck. The beacon was 29 feet high and the barrel of tar at the top of the post was reached by a series of projecting horizontal steps. The warning system was eventually tested by a trial lighting on the night of October 7th 1803 but there is no record of the result of the test.

Another part of the Elizabethan preparations, the removal of all food, was also adopted. Preparations were made in great detail. The length of the coast was divided into 13 small districts and a "Captain of the District" appointed. He was responsible for seeing to the removal of all the horses, cattle, sheep and in fact anything that could be of use to the enemy. He had to arrange for the removal of all grain and flour from his district to troop headquarters, and finally the Captain was responsible for burning all the stocks of wheat, barley and oats in his area, thus depriving the enemy of any food.

The military commander decided that the herds of cattle, flocks of sheep, the swine and the wagons of grain and flour from Holderness should all be driven across the River Hull to a place west of Beverley. The owners of the stock, etc., would be recompensed by the Government providing that the stock was driven off as arranged and that the owners had subsequently joined the local defence force.

To transport the women and children to safety wagons and carts were always to be held ready. In Patrington all the wagons were kept throughout the summer in the Market Place and it is possible that the wagons for the Hornsea people were kept in Hornsea Market Place too. Places in each wagon were allotted to an individual and instructions as to the clothes and food to be taken were written on a "Ticket of Removal." One of the Hornsea tickets is in the County Archives in Beverley. This says:-

Holderness Ticket of Removal
Township of Hornsea
You and 6 children belong to Waggon Letter B to which you are to repair as soon as possible, with a Change of Linen, and one Blanket for each Person, wrapped up in the Coverlid of Your Bed, and bring with you all the Food in your possession
Wm Jones Overseer.

The warning signal for the exodus of people and animals was to be the ringing of the church bells, which otherwise were not to be rung for services, together with the lighting of the beacons. The apprehensiveness felt by the population is conveyed by this account of one old lady on her nightly preparations for bed:-

"After taking off my spectables and tying them and my Bible in the special bundle, which lay near my bed head, I used to look across the country to Bainton Beacon to see if it was alight, for we were always

fearful that we should be aroused at night, because of the landing of the French, and hurried away to a more secure place."

In order to counter any French landings, the Militia regiments were embodied when war broke out in 1793. In peacetime, the Militia were part time soldiers who were chosen by lot. In time of war they served full time and their main purpose was home defence. In order to minimise desertion, Militia regiments rarely served in their own districts and so, in 1793 the York, East Riding Militia, including some Hornsea men, moved to the Norfolk coast. In its place came the Northumberland Militia, which established a camp on the slopes of Leys Hill on the Atwick road. The regiment served in Hornsea between 1793 and 1799 and was joined briefly by the Durham Militia, the Warwickshire Fencible Cavalry and the 5th York, West Riding Supplementary Militia. In order to reinforce the Militia, in 1794 the government authorised the formation of Volunteer units and it was decided that three companies should be raised to defend the East Riding coast, with one stationed at Bridlington, one at Patrington and the third at Hornsea. In the event, the Hornsea company never materialised because only two volunteers came forward.

More successful was Thomas Grimston of Kilnwick and Grimston Garth who formed the East Riding Gentlemen and Yeomanry Cavalry. This unit was about 60 strong and consisted mostly of men from Holderness, and its title gives an idea of the type of men who volunteered. Nevertheless, in order to fulfil his quota of recruits Grimston had to pay his men despite the volunteer nature of the unit. The money was raised from the contributions of supporters. In addition, the men would not serve until the title "East Yorkshire" was changed to "East Riding" in order to avoid service outside of their own locality.

As was appreciated by the military command, the Holderness coast was ideal for a landing of enemy troops, particularly near Spurn Point. Consequently large encampments of militia were established at Dimlington and Ridgemount together with small camps of militia at other sites along the coast including Hornsea.

Since the well-to-do maintained the habit of. "taking the Spa waters," in the summer months throughout the war, the advent of the gallant officers and men from the several Militia regiments would add to the gaiety of the season. No doubt many concerts and balls would be held in the town in the evenings, and of course during the day horse racing could be enjoyed on the sands of Hornsea Beck. The effect of the influx of high spirited young men in their bright uniforms on the young ladies of Hornsea can be judged by the entries in the parish register, which shows that between 1793 and 1799 there were thirteen marriages between Hornsea women and soldiers.

The Royal Navy too made preparations for the defence of the

coast. Companies of Sea Fencibles were raised from amongst the fishermen, pilots, bargees and sailors working in coastal waters to help form another warning system against the French. Since many of these same people were engaged in the very lucrative business of smuggling in connivance with the French it was an equivocal situation. The Navy was also in the habit of using press gangs to search the coastal villages for recruits for the Navy. They were entitled to take any able-bodied men not already in the Militia or otherwise exempt from service.

From March 1802 to May 1803 Britain and France were at peace and most of the Militia and Volunteer units were stood down. When war broke out again a new recruiting drive began and by October 1803 Hornsea and the parishes around had managed to raise a unit called the North Holderness Volunteer Infantry. The establishment was 6 officers and 134 men and the company was commanded by Captain Richard Bethell of Catfoss.

In 1803 signal stations were set up at Paull, Spurn, Dimlington, Hornsea and Flamborough. Strongpoints were also built that summer at Hilston, Hornsea and Dimlington.

In 1804 Napoleon Bonaparte became Emperor of the French and invasion forces massed along the Channel coast. The fear of Bonaparte, or "Boney" as he was commonly called, was a very real one for country people. The children were warned by anxious parents not to play far from home or "Boney" would get them.

The Battle of Trafalgar in 1805 put paid to Napoleon's scheme to invade Britain, but the Militia and Volunteers remained in being. In 1808 the passing of the Local Militia Act was the means of raising permanent local Militia from all able-bodied men between 18 and 40; they would serve in their own counties for short periods, never more than 28 days, a year. The 3rd Battalion East Riding Local Militia, which was based in Beverley, absorbed the North Holderness Volunteers.

There are no details of the enrollment of Hornsea men in this local militia but Withernsea has two items in the Overseers Accounts of 1811:-

The loackal mileto waran 1.9
Paid to the men inrolled in the local mileto £3. 0. 0

After the defeat of Napoleon in 1815 the Local Militia ceased training in 1816 and was disbanded in 1836. The original York, East Riding Militia Regiment remained in being, although between 1817 and 1851 it was only called out four times.

12 Smuggling in and around Hornsea

The idea of a tax on commodities coming into the country was introduced into England in 1643. Although there had been since the 13th century a tariff duty on the export of hides and wool, this had been mainly to encourage the English manufacture of woollen and leather goods and to discourage the flow of the finest raw material in Europe to the Continent rather than to raise money. The new excise tax was levied on many goods, but the largest part of the revenue came from the tax on alcohol and tobacco - "Brandy for the parson, baccy for the clerk," of the poem, and this remained the case until the permanent imposition of income tax in 1842. The twenty years of the French Revolutionary and Napoleonic Wars were also the heyday of the smuggler and it is this period which has attracted so many stories and legends.

The duty of preventing the illegal importation of alcohol and tobacco into the country without the payment of tax was that of the Customs and Excise Board. Headquarters were in London, and the Holderness district came under the authority of the Collector in Hull, and his area of jurisdiction was known as the Creek of Hull. Amongst the staff listed as working in the Customs in Hull were Surveyors, Port Gaugers, Landwaiters, Coastwaiters, Searchers and Boatmen. Judging by the list of privateers and letters of marque captured by the Customs officers, they were reasonably efficient in preventing smuggling into the port.

The men and officers appointed by the Board were very conscious of the importance of their task and there is almost a crusading spirit to be found in the earliest letters between the Collectors and the Board. Their fulminations against, "run goods," as contraband cargoes were called, contrasts markedly with the attitude of the captains of the ships running the goods. The determination of the captains to elude detection is shown in one of the first letters written to the Collector in Hull in 1722:-

"It is the Practice of the Mas' of Ships to Leave out of this first Report a considerable part of their Loading and when ye Goods are discovered to be on Board then to make a second report of what shall be discovered and where ships have been hindered from running Goods omitted in ye report they have made a third or fourth Report. You are to prosecute for the penalty of £500 for making a false report."

In 1732 H.M.S. *"The Fly"* was appointed to cruise between Flamborough Head and Yarmouth to prevent smuggling and, "... to help prevent the Exportation of the Woollen Manufacture of the Kingdom to Foreign Parts." The nearest capture to Holderness seems to have been that of a privateer off Scarborough in 1744.

On land, there were in Holderness only six men to supervise the coastline from Bridlington to Spurn Point and inland as far west as Howden. The low clay cliffs and the sandy beaches provided an ideal terrain for the landing of smuggled goods. The sparsity of villages along the coast meant that detection was very unlikely even with the co-operation of the villagers, but in fact the villagers were wholeheartedly on the side of the smugglers. The lack of success of the affairs in the detection of smuggling led to the Board In London directing in 1755:-

"... that orders be given to the Officers to exchange stations and to enjoin them to be more careful and active in the execution of their expected Duty than they have hitherto been."

In this changeover John Wright became Riding Surveyor between Hull and Howden, George Wright, Surveyor between Spurn Head and Bridlington, Edward Bee and B. Garwood at Patrington, Barnabas Prickett at Aldbrough and Henry Spendlove at Barton upon Humber, Lincolnshire. Having received further directives from the Board urging greater activity, Bedell, the Chief Officer in Hull, writes in July 1755:-

"We acquaint your Honours that four years ago, having a great reason to suspect the Smuggling Trade being carried on upon the Coast of Holderness, we Excited the Officers to be Vigilant and a stop was put thereto. And at present we have no cause of suspicion that any Fraudulent practices are in like manner carried on, but upon this particular occasion we have recommended diligent and faithful Execution of Duty to the several officers."

The fact remained that no matter how "Diligent' and 'Excited" an officer was, it needed an army of watchers to be effective in Holderness, and with only six officers for the area it was impossible to succeed in combating the smuggling. A more accurate picture of the situation is given in the Hull Packet and Humbrian Gazette in 1787:-

"Not withstanding the large seizure lately made here every post brings fresh accounts of long wool being smuggled off by the French from the neighbouring coast. No less than three vessels were lately seen at one time plying off and on between Boston Deeps and the Humber. The vessels glut the country with brandy, cheat the revenue and return

loaded to France with the staple commodity of our country and unless a
speedy stop is put to this practice our manufactory must be ruined and
thousands of our poor workmen must be turned adrift to starve. Long
wool has risen considerably very lately occasioned by the smuggling
carried on to France."

Not surprisingly, the producers of, "... the staple commodity of
our country," had a different point of view. In 1788 a meeting was held
of the gentlemen, clergy and occupiers of lands in the East Riding to
consider the implication of a Bill lately presented to Parliament for
preventing the exportation of wool. Amongst those present were William
Bethell of Rise and Marmaduke Constable of Wassand. The meeting
resolved that a petition against the Bill be presented on the grounds
that it would interfere with sheep breeding.

Although the stringency of the continental blockade was
increased during the course of the French Revolutionary and Napoleonic
Wars, this highly profitable illegal trade between the two belligerent
nations was maintained. When in the summer of 1798 a company of
Sea Fencibles was raised by the Royal Navy from the sailors, fishermen,
pilots and bargees of the area for the purpose of patrolling coastal
waters, the recruits would in all probability have been those most
actively engaged in the smuggling trade.

The extent of the support the smugglers received from local
people was perfectly understood by General Howard Vyse, the
commanding officer of Militia in Holderness. In 1807 he wrote an
illuminating account to headquarters:-

*"There are agents established who direct all the different branches of this
illegal traffic and who on the arrival of any of the smuggling vessels off
the coast send immediate but secret notice around the Country to all the
different description of persons concerned in carrying on the smuggling
business, who assemble at the Landing Places pointed out to them. As soon
as the Smuggling vessel arrives at the rendezvous the cargo is either
brought on shore by his own boats, assisted by the fishing cobles of the
place or is taken away by those cobles to some more private and more
convenient landing place, from where a large proportion of the smuggled
goods is carried immediately to the interior of the country through some of
the numerous and little-frequented paths.*

*The remainder of the smuggled goods which cannot, on first being landed,
be thus disposed of is secreted till an opportunity offers of dispersing it in
small qualities to the Inhabitants of the Towns and Villages upon the
Coast. I am well assured that every facility is given to the Smugglers, not
only by almost all the lower classes of people but likewise (I am sorry to*

add) by many whose fortune and rank in life cannot allow them to plead either necessity or want as an excuse for subverting the Law or defrauding the Revenue of their Country."

One of the few records of the capture of contraband goods off Holderness does, in fact, concern a well-known East Riding family. At Bridlington in 1768:-

"... a Coastwatcher stopped and lodged in His Majesty's warehouse from aboard the 'Neptune' from Liverpool one cased Pipe supposed to contain Madeira Wine and a small Box containing a few pieces Liverpool China and a few Potts of Pickles for want of a sufferance of Coast despatch. We humbly inform that the Pipe and Box are both directed for Sir George Strickland."

However, the General's strictures could have been equally applied to his own troops since it was impossible to station the Militia in one district for more than three days before the smugglers had succeeded in subverting them, according to report.

Hornsea

The man responsible for patrolling the coast of Holderness was called a Riding Surveyor and as Hornsea was so central, a customs officer was stationed there from 1720 onwards. There is an entry in the Manor Court Rolls for that year when, "Robert Smithson, Custom House Officer," bought a cottage in Southgate. An officer was stationed at Hornsea from 1720 to 1840 and several of them were well enough accepted by the community to be members of the jury of the manor court. Their days must have been spent in endlessly patrolling the clifftops in all seasons, observing all the changes of tides and weather as part of their job. No wonder that the effect of coastal erosion at Hornsea could be noted down in detail for Poulson the historian by Mr. Joseph Harrison, "Head Officer of H.M. Customs for Yorkshire, sometime collector of H.M. Customs in Boston, North America."

There is only one reference in the letter book of the Customs Board to a local case and this is in a letter dated December 14th 1732:-

"We received your letter of the 8th Inst. transmitting the affidavit of Mr. Legard, Officer at Hornsea, relating to his being obstructed and threatened to be fired at in searching the house of John Herbert at Mapleton for Run Goods, for which Abuse the said Herbert is committed to Gaol and having advised thereon with our Solicitor he has Reported there is sufficient Proof

to Prosecute the said Herbert. And we direct you agreeable to his Opinion to imploy the Attorney concerned for the Crown to attend the sessions with the witness and get an Indictment."

By a strange coincidence the only known case of smuggled goods being landed in Hornsea took place in the same month, on December 23rd 1732. During the period from 1721 to 1831 there was no vicar resident in Hornsea and only a visiting curate to preach on some Sundays. To anyone in search of a large, dry, safe and unsupervised place of storage, the crypt of Hornsea church was a perfect place of concealment. It seems that on the night of December 23rd there was a freak storm, a hurricane, which travelled across the centre of Hornsea and cut a path of destruction 240 yards across, having the church as its centre, in its journey to the sea. The events of that December night are described in a letter written by a Hornsea man and given later to the historian, Poulson:-

"The vault has been used formerly as a place to conceal smuggled goods in. I have heard that the late Parish Clerk was concealing prohibited goods there in the night of 23rd Dec. 1732, the very time when the violent hurricane came and unroofed the Church, the door having been opened by the clerk for that design. George ----'s (a noted smuggler upon the coast) ship was certainly near the beck that night and was laid flat on her side during the time the tempest continued which was only two minutes. The Parish Clerk was suddenly afflicted with a paralytic stroke which deprived him of the use of his speech and confined him to his bed for some months before his death. We are not authorized to declare the course of God's judgments but this hurricane a few centuries ago would have been deemed so."

If Poulson thought it more discreet to omit the smuggler's surname it is possible that the family was still living in the vicinity. In the Manor Court Rolls some years after 1732 is a brief mention, "George Gallaway, mariner died at sea." The Gallaway family owned several cottages at Hornsea Beck for many generations, and a John Gallaway, "panierman", had given evidence at the Inquisition of 1608. The family were still living in Hornsea in the mid-19th century, when a Jonathan Gallaway, a veterinary surgeon, lived in the house in Westgate now called Gallaway Lodge.

The unfortunate parish clerk was said to have died some months after that December. According to the parish register only two men died in 1733. A butcher, John Greensides died in August, and William Foster, maltman in July. William Foster owned the White House in Southgate which at that time was an inn, ideal cover for the possession of smuggled spirits. The stream alongside might enable a small boat to be rowed in from the sea and offer every facility to the smugglers.

As well as the church crypt, the smugglers of the day found the

67

mills of the area useful for storing the boxes and barrels of their trade. There were two windmills in Hornsea at this time. Concealment amongst the sacks of grain and flour was easy and the constant traffic of carts and horses to and from the mill would allow the run goods to be carried in daylight. The sand cadgers transporting sand, gravel and cobbles from the beach in panniers slung on either side of a donkey's back would be another means of carrying the goods to their customers. There is no doubt that smuggling was a very well organized operation and a profitable one, too. The majority of the villagers, who had a subsistence standard of living, welcomed the opportunity of earning the large sums of money the smugglers had to offer for a very little work. One old lady, speaking many years later, said that around 1820 most of the villagers in Kilnsea had a hand in smuggling. Since the customs officers were always vigilant the utmost secrecy was necessary to protect the contraband trade. There seems to have been only one occasion when this secrecy was broken. In 1837 a Hornsea farm labourer called Baker was on trial accused of murdering by poison a farmer called King who lived at Trinity Farm, Hornsea Burton. The most suspicious circumstance against Baker, who worked on Mr. King's farm, was his possession of a large sum of money, the wage of a farm labourer being then around £15 a year. Frightened for his life, Baker was forced to confess that he had been given nearly £90 by the smugglers for assisting them to land cargoes nearby.

After the permanent imposition of income tax in 1842, the customs duty on spirits and tobacco was very much reduced and therefore smuggling was no longer the profitable business it had been.

"Pennel the Pyrate"

A document of some interest to Hornsea was retrieved from a bonfire of old papers near Hornsea Burton by Mr. William Stephenson some time in the middle of the 19th century.

The document begins:-

"Recd March 22d 1772 of William Brough, Esq. By the hand of Mr. John Crickitt Thirty Seven pounds in full for the within Account contracted by the late Deputy Marshall Mr. Charles Douglas Bowden."

William Brough of Rolston Hall was Marshall of the High Court of Admiralty, which dealt with maritime crimes and the document lists the expenses incurred in connection with the executions of criminals between May 1762 and December 1771. The entry of interest to Hornsea is the one for the execution of Edward Pennel and others.

1769	For the Execution of Edwd Pennel and five others			
Nvr 26	To 6 Men Cleaning the Shore a tide		18.	
	To 6 Men ditto ditto		18.	
27	To 8 Men 2 Tides each cleaning ye shore	2.	8.	
28	To 8 Men ditto	2.	8.	
	To watching the Gallows in the night		4.	6.
29	To 4 Men 2 Tides each	1.	4.	
	To 2 Deals 6 Sparrs and Spike Nails		16.	6.
	To 3 New Shovells, etc.		6.	
	To Putting up the gallows and taking it down	2.		
		£11.	3.	

Pennel had been the ringleader of a mutiny aboard a ship sailing off the Holderness coast. The mutineers had murdered the captain and sank the vessel near Hornsea. Rowing themselves ashore, they landed in Hornsea. In "The Folk Lore of East Yorkshire" published in 1890, John Nicholson says:-

"Through quarelling while drunk, their crime was discovered and they were arrested. Pennel was tried at York, found guilty, and sentenced to be hanged on Hornsea Gibbet. Here his body hung in chains fully dressed even to the buckles on his shoes, until someone more venturesome than the rest, stole the buckles."

Nicholson goes on to say that the name "Hornsea Pennels" was given to a poaching, loafing lot of vagabonds.

However, Poulson, writing 50 years earlier, says -

"A gibbet formerly stood on Hornsea Common, on which had been suspended the body of a notorious pirate and smuggler, named Pennel, who murdered his captain and sunk the vessell near Hornsea. He was tried in London and the body sent down from thence in a case marked 'glass.' It was prepared for the disgusting exhibition by being bound with iron hoops and in 1770 hung up on the North Cliff, which with its ornament, is now washed away."

In the records of the Court of Oyer and Terminer of the Admiralty are details of the trials of several of the men on the list of executions found in Hornsea Burton. Pennel is not one of them; this may indicate that he was in fact tried in York although the records of the court are far from orderly and his trial papers could have been lost, It seems certain from the list found in Hornsea Burton that Pennel was in fact executed in London as were certainly the other men, including the notorious West Country pirate, John Wynn. The method of execution was to tie down the pirate on the shore between the High and Low Water mark and let him drown. The number of tides his body was left was according to the seriousness of his crimes. The corpse was then hung on a gallows as a warning for all to see. The body of Pennel must have hung in London from November until the end of April when it was shipped to Hornsea. Although Poulson refers to a gibbet on "Hornsea Common" the gibbet was on the coast. According to an entry in the parish register, "1770 in May Pennel the Pyrate hung in chains in Beacon Close near Hornsea Beck." Beacon Close lies now north of the Marine Hotel and some 300 yards out to sea.

The finding of the document in Hornsea Burton is a little mysterious, as William Brough lived at Rolston Hall. However, land and a cottage in Hornsea Burton on which Smithson's Rent Charges were paid was owned in 1833 by a Mrs. Brough of Rolston, and it may have been that old documents belonging to the Brough family were being burnt on the bonfire in Hornsea Burton when the above mentioned list was retrieved.

The door to the crypt under St. Nicholas' Church. Local tradition maintains that smuggled goods were stored here until such time that transport inland could be arranged. On 23rd December 1732 it was reported that the parish clerk was in the crypt when the church was unroofed by a violent storm. Probably fearing Divine retribution, the man was rendered speechless and died not long afterwards.

13 The Enclosure of the Open Fields

The open field system of agriculture, begun probably in Anglo-Saxon times, lasted in England for nearly one thousand years. However, throughout this period the system was in the process of adaptation and change. For example, while the scattered distribution of an individual's strips of land in the open fields ensured an equitable share of the best and worst soils, it could be an inconvenience to have to move from one strip to another when working on the land. So there was often a tendency to consolidate strips into larger areas of land. In addition, the more ambitious farmers, who wished to utilise more advanced or experimental methods, could be held back by having to conform to communal decisions as to what to grow. Thus, there was a increasing tendency for farmers to try to have their land ideally in one piece. They could then enclose their land with a fence or hedge and farm it as they wished. These early enclosures were usually by agreement and were often carried out in a piecemeal fashion. An example of this is the township of Hornsea Burton which was enclosed by agreement in 1663. Enclosures were put on a more legal footing from the beginning of the 17th century, when enclosures could be facilitated by Act of Parliament. The movement reached its height between 1750 and 1845, at a time when Parliament was dominated by country landowners who wished to take advantage of new farming techniques and exploit their land to the full. However, those whose claim to work land in the open fields was merely traditional, could be forced to become into landless labourers. In addition, those whose allotment of land was very small and not enough to support a family, might be forced to sell and either work as labourers for other owners, or take their chances in industrial towns, or even emigrate. The enclosures had a tremendous effect on the rural population because although about one third of the population had moved into the towns by the middle of the 18th century, two thirds still lived in villages and had their living from the land.

Up to the time of the enclosures the major settlements in the East Riding were on the coast or along the foot of the Wolds. In Holderness, which was very badly drained, only $1/3$ of the land, the easiest to cultivate, was under the plough. The chief crops were wheat, oats and beans with some barley and a very little rye. Roots were not a successful innovation because of the heavy clay soil but another factor was the reluctance of Holderness farmers to try new crops.

In Holderness the enclosure of the open fields began with Catwick in 1731 and by 1810 all the village lands were enclosed except for

Mappleton and Kilnsea both of which were finally enclosed in 1843.

Hornsea before enclosure, like 80% of Holderness, had a two field system of crop rotation because the heavy clay soil needed longer as pasture to renew fertility. Again, like in most of the villages, the two Hornsea fields were named after the points of the compass - the East Field and the West Field. Southorpe villagers however, chose to call their fields Far Field and Hither Field. (Sometimes the latter was called Southorpe Field.)

The decision to enclose the Hornsea town fields was reached at a meeting on August 16th 1800 which was attended by the twelve most important land owners. Notice of this meeting was pinned on the church door on August 17th, 24th and 31st. A series of meetings was held from September to December 1800 when the details of the area of the town fields, the price per oxgang of compensation and other details of future policy were settled. It was agreed that there were 81 oxgangs of land in Hornsea Fields calculated as containing 16 acres per oxgang giving a total of about 1304 acres. There were also some 400 acres used as permanent pasture land in the Leys along Atwick Road and the Brockhams and other pieces along the Seaton Road. There were also said to be about 300 acres of old enclosures in Hornsea and Southorpe. The two Southorpe fields were said to contain 24 oxgangs calculated at 24 acres each, giving a total of 576 acres. This would seem to indicate that the Southorpe land was much easier to work than the Hornsea land since one oxgang was the amount of land that one ox could plough in a year. The details of the working of the Southorpe fields showed how wasteful of land was the open field system, because out of every 24 acres two acres was allowed as headlands or land ends to give access to the strips of land.

One suggestion for the future was that a strip of land 150 yards wide running down the cliff edge in the Hornsea East Field should be left as common pasture and stocked with cattle. This idea was not acted upon but the strip of land was ultimately divided into 30 parallel strips of varying widths running east and west.

At the next meeting on January 2nd 1801 a petition to the House of Commons was signed by the twelve leading land holders including Charlotte Bethell, Peter Acklom, Cornwell Baron Wilson, and Marmaduke Constable. This petition asked that the town fields of Hornsea containing about 1500 acres be enclosed, and that permission be given to, "... divide, allot and inclose the open fields, ings, pastures, common and waste grounds." The Bill was read on the 8th and 12th May and the Royal Assent was given on June 11th 1801.

The commissioners chosen to adjudge the awards of land were Peter Jackson, Joseph Dickinson and John Lee and they held their first meeting at the New Inn, (now the Pike and Heron,) on July 19th 1801. Their first task was to allow those who claimed to own land in Hornsea to stake their claims. They also issued instructions that until the final awards were made, the traditional way of farming was to continue.

The commissioners seemed to have followed a system of holding a meeting in Hornsea at the New Inn and then the following meeting at the Tiger Inn, Beverley where any complaints about the decision could be heard. This of course meant a 15 mile walk for the poorer land claimants if they had a complaint to make. The minutes of the meetings have a list of people present but these never included the smaller landowners. Either they did not attend the meetings, which seems extraordinary in view of the fact that their one asset, their holdings, were being valued or they were not considered important enough to be remembered.

The two town fields of Hornsea at the time of enclosure ran from the Atwick parish boundary in the north to Eastgate and Westgate and from the cliff edge of the East Field west to the parish boundary with Seaton, which was the western edge of the West Field. Previously a strip of land along the Seaton boundary had not been cultivated regularly but left as rough pasture and parts were still called North Moor and South Moor at enclosure. (In the terrier of the church lands in this area are listed strips called Hart Hill, Furzebush and Brackendale, which would seem to confirm more recent cultivation.) It is possible that this land was taken into cultivation after 1661, for an agreement in the Manor Court Rolls was made then between six holders of land in the West Field to make a pathway, and this pathway is again mentioned in 1750 when land, "... near Aram gate called Nor Moor Path," is mentioned. Northorpe as a hamlet seems to have existed up to 1732 when a cottage was surrendered, but in 1780 it is referred to in the Manor Court Rolls as the Northorpe oxgang and it was probably after 1780 that for the greater convenience of working the land, the North Field was divided off from the northern end of the West Field.

The original area of the common land of Hornsea was around the edge of the Mere from Foss Dyke, (which formed the boundary between Hornsea common land and Southorpe common,) all the way along the East end of the Mere at the back of the town and on either side of the Seaton Road. The area of common on the north side of the Seaton Road was in three parts called the Meany Piece, the Martles and the Brockhams. The far end of the Brockhams was marked by the Brockham, or Brockholme Stone, (which is still in place,) and there was also a gateway there to fence off the crops from straying animals. After 1717 a strip of land on either side of the Atwick Road was kept as permanent pasture, being known henceforth in the Manor Court Rolls as Hornsea Leys.

In 1801, the year of the Act of Enclosure, there were 533 people living in 126 dwellings according to the census returns for Hornsea. The only streets in the town were still just Southgate, Newbegin, Market Place, Westgate together with Back Westgate, (first mentioned in the Manor Court Rolls in 1705,) and Eastgate which had been extended in

1653 down to the Chrystills. Outside of the town the roadways were unfenced wide tracks and a traveller would have to pick the best way through the ruts and potholes, for the road was only sparsely surfaced with gravel or small stones. North of the town was the road across the town fields to Atwick and South of it was the road to Rolston. Lelley Lane led from the end of Southgate to Southorpe Hill and there was only a footbridge over Stream Dyke in Southgate until 1800 when a wider bridge was built. As well as the road to Seaton over the Common, there was also a roadway which led from the corner of Westgate and Atwick Road across the West Field to Arram or "Ergham" as it was often spelt.

Some Details of the Working of the Fields

Up to, and even some years after the enclosure, agricultural methods were still primitive. Bedell said that seed was still being sown broadcast by hand in 1847 and that grain was still threshed with a flail. The drainage of the town fields was improved by the use of a town plough, an implement of great size drawn by a team of two horses and six oxen. Working under the supervision of the byelawmen, this town plough made deep furrows which led away the surface water into a ditch. From the list of church fees in 1764 it seems it was the custom that a charge of two sheaves of wheat from every oxgang in the town fields was paid to the parish clerk for ringing the church bell in Harvest time at six in the morning and six in the evening.

Joseph Lambert, the Quaker, was spokesman for the smaller tenants and gave details of the animals that they claimed to run on the town's pastures in a letter written to Joseph Dickinson on March 11th 1801:-

> "I have presumed to throw some hints before thee, because thou has not been present at all the meetings with thy colleagues and I thought perhaps thou might not have seen our joint claims which was for all geese, pigs and five sheep free in the average fields for the winter half year and the further stray of such stock as was likely for a cottager to have (say three gates or more). Also that the farmers stocked in common and could not lett any gates prior to the fields being cut and mode of culture altered. Many who have benefited by the aforesaid privilige to the amount of 30/- or 40/- annually, for instance some at times have only a flock of geese and a pig then again a sow and her Board, sometimes two Board and frequently as many as three cows, or a horse and cow or two horses."

The expression, "three gates or more" referred to the amount of grassland each cottager was entitled to on the Leys. The church terrier

74

of 1764 says that the church was entitled to, "... 2 horses gates and $4/5$ of another in the Leys, that is to say 3 acres, 2 roods and 6 perches," and this seems to indicate that each "gate" was slightly over one acre.

From Lambert's letter it seems that each cottager claimed three gates of pasture and common on which to run 3 cows or horses, five sheep together with a sow and her board as well as a flock of geese. Lambert's letter goes on to describe other advantages the cottager could claim from the town fields.

> "... some who keep a horse and a little cart for useful purposes, the little free common with a trifle of help was summer pasturage and the winter they was of great service having had liberty also to cut grass between the lands and the furrows."

The Enclosure Awards

Eight years after the passing of the Enclosure Act for Hornsea, the awards were finally enrolled and a map drawn up to show them in November 1809. The awards were measured in the traditional units of acres, roods and (square) perches.

Measurement of Land
30¼ square yards = 1 square perch
40 square perches = 1 Rood
4 roods = 1 acre or 4840 square yards

In total, 62 individuals were awarded land in the enclosure of Hornsea and Southorpe. Eleven of these persons were allotted 71% of the land between them, while 23 people were awarded 5 acres or less each.

Hornsea Enclosure Awards
Principal Allotments
(Measured in acres, roods and perches)
Philip Blundell, esq. on behalf of his wife, Catherine, 354-3-32

Mrs. Blundell was the Lay Improprietor of the Tithes. During the Middle Ages, everyone had to give one tenth of everything to the church in order to support the priest, keep up the building and provide for the poor. Where churches, (like Hornsea,) belonged to monasteries, they often appropriated most of the tithes to themselves and put in a Vicar, who only received a small part of the tithes. When the monasteries were dissolved, their tithes were claimed by the Crown, which then sold the right to gather tithes for a lump sum. The tithes were often sold to laymen who then became Lay Improprietors, and often had no connections with the places from where they received the tithes. The tithes, which were often converted to cash payments, could be bought, sold, bequeathed and inherited like any other property. For example, when the Act of Parliament for the enclosure of Hornsea was passed in 1801, the Lay Improprietor was Michael Newton, Esq., but by 1809 Catherine Blundell had taken over. She might have been Michael Newton's daughter, but research has failed to find any family connection. At the time of the enclosure it was decided to do away with tithes, (which was not unusual,) but the Improprietor had to be compensated for loss of income and Mr. Newton insisted on land, thus causing Mrs. Blundell to receive the largest award of all.

Mrs. Charlotte Bethell of Rise, Lady of the Manor, 253-3-36
Hugh Bethell of Rise (1691-1752) bought land at Hornsea and the title of Lord of the Manor for £5,000 in 1743 from the Acklam family. His son, William (1728-1799) married Charlotte Pennyman (1735-1814) but they had no children. William decreed in his will that Charlotte was to inherit the whole of his estates and enjoy them for the rest of her life. Hence her title of Lady of the Manor and allocation of land. When she died in 1814 the Bethell estates were inherited by Richard Bethell whom William had adopted as his son and heir, although there is no known family connection.

Marmaduke Constable, esq., of Wassand, 233-2-36
He was allotted most of the former common land on the borders of Hornsea Mere, the lake which his family had owned for generations.

Bryan Taylor, esq., of Bridlington, 130-1-12

Peter Acklom, esq., of North Newbald, 125-1-24
He was probably related to the Quaker family which had been important in Hornsea in the 17th and early 18th centuries.

John Kirkus, gent., of Beverley, 109-1-0
He amassed his allotment by buying out owners of small plots.

William Whitfield, gent., of Beverley, 102-1-4
Like most of these larger owners he had no real stake in Hornsea and by 1804 he had mortgaged the land to a Bainton farmer for £600.

Cornwell Baron Wilson, husbandman of Hornsea, 99-2-14
This is the first of the larger owners who belonged to Hornsea and who was directly involved in farming.

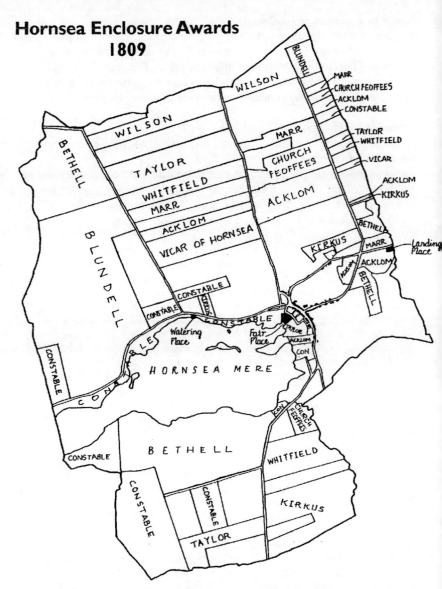

Hornsea Enclosure Awards 1809

Note: Only the larger allotments are named. The blank areas contain either old enclosures or small plots. The remaining common land is shaded in black.

Vicar of Hornsea, 67-3-24
As part of their stipend, vicars were permitted to receive a small share of the tithes, (or all of the tithes if they were rectors.) The Vicar of Hornsea received 43 acres of his allotment in lieu of tithes. The rest of the land belonged to the glebe, which was land allocated to parish priests either to farm themselves, or pay someone to farm for them or rent out.

Thomas Marr, gent., of Skidby, 67-2-12

Feoffees of Hornsea Church, 61-2-12
At some indeterminate time in the past some land had been bequeathed to the parish church. This land was rented out and the money used for the upkeep of the building. The land and money were administered by a committee known as the Feoffees, which still exists today.

Besides these larger awards there were 23 awards of less than five acres; indeed nearly half the awards were of less than 10 acres. The smallest award went to Thomas Myass, yeoman of Hornsea, who was allotted just 20 square perches, or 605 square yards of land. If this had been an actual square it would have measured about 75x75 feet. Many owners of the small plots could not provide for their families by farming, so they often sold the land to larger owners. In addition, the owners of the land all had to contribute towards the cost of the enclosure but many small owners could not afford the fees and had to sell their small plots. The initial valuation of the land was about £10 an oxgang, (16 acres,) in Hornsea. This would mean that in return for surrendering their rights to the land the villagers received sums which were inadequate to secure alternative means of earning a living. A class of landless labourers grew up, who either worked on the land for others, or moved into industrial towns like Hull. The more enterprising of the villagers emigrated to Canada and America to seek a new life. A footnote to the census figures of 1831 states that nearly one hundred persons had lately emigrated to America. Again in the 1841 census is a note that a large number of people had emigrated since December 1840. Altogether 33 houses out of 187 in the town were uninhabited at that time. As the agricultural workers left the town the proportion of those working in trades or serving the seasonal visitors rose until by 1841 there were only 56 workers in agriculture as against 76 in the manufacturing trades and 56 in other trades. The numbers of unsupported poor increased in Hornsea and other parishes so that in 1834 several parishes combined to build the Union Workhouse at Skirlaugh.

The appearance of the countryside changed completely. The roads to Beverley, to Atwick and to Southorpe were fenced off and hedges planted either side. A road to Bewholme was made across the West Field and Cliff Lane made to give access to the cliffside strips from Eastgate. The enclosure allotments were bordered by hawthorn hedges and divided into fields by more hedges. Those farmers, either as owners or, more likely as tenants, whose land was away from the centre of population, were encouraged to build a farm house on the land, which gave rise to the country landscape with its scattered farms which we see today. With the enclosures the large amounts of capital needed for the drainage of the land become available and by the mid-19th century the area under the plough had doubled.

Only a tiny amount of the former common land remained. Sea Road, (nowadays known unofficially as Little Eastgate,) was to extend Eastgate down to the sea where a one acre landing place was to be made. Two acres of common land to be known as Fair Place was to be held in trust by Mrs. Bethell and a 20 square perch area on the north bank of the Mere was allotted as a watering place for animals.

Appendix
Hornsea & Hornsea Burton Farmers in 1851

George & Edward Bennett	Old Hall	150 acres
William Bird	Eastfield	150 acres
William Bulson	Southgate	100 acres Also butcher
Robert Byas	Southgate	140 acres
Thomas Dukes	Mount Pleasant	15 acres
Joseph Eldin	Hornsea Burton	60 acres Also brick maker
John Gallaway	Westgate	9 acres
William Harmon	Eastgate	200 acres
William Harper	Newbegin	18 acres Also carrier
Henry Heron	Back Westgate	101 acres
Robert Heron	Back Westgate	100 acres
John Heslop	Old Hotel	85 acres Also innkeeper
William Hodgson	Victoria Hotel	38 acres Also innkeeper
William Hornsey	Hornsea Burton	67 acres
Mary King	Trinity House Farm	80 acres
William Lowsbro'	Newbegin	20 acres Also cartman
William Pexton	Southorpe	144 acres
John Simpson	Brockholme	356 aces
Samuel Simpson	Westgate	188 acres
David Smales	Mereside	9 acres Also joiner
Ann Stillingfleet	Southorpe	204 acres
William Straker	New Hotel	50 acres Also innkeeper
William Tranmer	Northfield	61 acres
William Walker	Hornsea Burton	71 acres
John Warcup	Bewholme Lane	56 acres

14 The Coming of the Chapels

The Independents, (later Congregationalists)

At the time of the Civil War in the 1640's Hull was a centre of dissent and played a leading role in the contest against the King and the Established Church. Other places in the East Riding which had enthusiastic dissenters were Rowley near Beverley, where a whole village left England to settle in Massachusetts, America, and Bridlington which had an Independent chapel in 1662. It may be that a dissenter is referred to in a Hornsea Manor Court Rolls entry of 1699 when, "Robert Richardson, Minister," buys a cottage in Newbegin.

One of the most vital Independent chapels in Hull was the Fish Street Chapel. It was a minister from this chapel, the Reverend George Lambert, who visited Hornsea in 1798, to spend a few days in the fashionable new pursuit of sea bathing. Having seen the state of religion in Hornsea at that time he decided there was, "work for the Gospel," there. Hornsea in fact was not at that time the only place needing spiritual guidance. Fellow evangelists of the Independent Chapel reported on the, "desolate district of Holderness," in the following terms:-

> *"We see not the hells and gin palaces and brothels of the Metropolis but fornication abounds; (the village green is the scene of many a brutal conflict) the village ale house resounds with the song of the drunkard, ribaldry and blasphemy."*

One place singled out for special mention was, "wicked Skipsea," but the whole area they felt needed to be reconverted.

Lambert was staying in rooms in a small cottage and with the permission of the owner he preached to a small group of people there. In the first minute book of the chapel is a reference to the difficult early days of the small band of converts:-

> *"The attempt was made and for a short time attendance was given but by the force of prejudice, unbelief, enmity to the gospel and persecution these messengers of mercy were obliged to desist for a time. But God who hears the prayers of his people was pleased in Mercy to open the heart of one of the inhabitants to receive Jesus by faith who soon after*

The person in whose house the meetings were held was called John Scaife and he lived in a cobble cottage in Newbegin now used as a café, (named "Cappuccino" in 2002.) His mother, a widow, rented some church land in Newbegin which provided a rent for repairing the parish cottages. The first five members of the new Church were Thomas March, Sam Hebblethwaite, Welham Mitchell, John Scaife and Jane March This small group of converts was helped in its desire to form a congregation by visits from members of the Fish Street Chapel who visited the neighbourhood and instructed people in houses and barns as they found the opportunity. By 1807 it was felt that enough converts had been made to warrant the building of a chapel and a gift of £25 to the Hornsea people was made by the Fish Street Mission.

It is interesting to compare the details of the gifts made by this Mission to the Holderness district:-

Skipsea Chapel	1801	Cost £90, sub £40, remainder £50
Coniston	1802	Schoolroom
Patrington	1802	Chapel cost £150, remainder £150
Long Riston	1803	Barn fitting up £10
Swine	1804	Room £16
Hornsea	1808	Chapel cost £465, sub £25, remainder £440
Leven	1809	Chapel cost £70, sub £35, remainder £35
Brandesburton	1809	Chapel cost £70, sub £35, remainder £35
Beeford	1810	Chapel cost £100, sub £40, remainder £60
Foston	1815	Chapel cost £280, sub £100, remainder £180
Frodingham	1820	Chapel cost £160, sub £133, remainder £27

It is obvious that Hornsea was the most ambitious project and that the finances of the new chapel would be heavily burdened for the first years of its existence. Chronologically this chapel was the first purpose-built nonconformist chapel in Hornsea although it belonged to the second of the dissenting congregations to be formed. (The Quakers were the first.)

Very suitably the foundation stone of the new Bethesda Chapel in Southgate was laid on November 13th 1807 by John Scaife, who had opened his house for meetings. At the opening service which took place in July 1808 the preacher in the morning was the Reverend Lambert who rode over from Hull. He described the occasion in the following words:-

"After preaching the lecture last night and rising soon after four o'clock this morning I went to Hornsea to the opening of a new place of worship. Preached in the forenoon. Brother Arundel spoke in the afternoon and Brother Hobson in the

*evening. It is a peculiar pleasure and has a promising
aspect to see so many tents set up for God as is the case at
present,* (referring to the number of chapels newly opened in
the area,) *and it gives me peculiar satisfaction to have seen
it at Hornsea."*

He then goes on to describe the Methodist services in Hornsea at
the time of his visit in 1798 and his wish to preach there too and
concludes:-

*"I spoke both parts of the day in the rooms I had taken for
lodgings and was well attended. The people discovered an
ardent desire to have someone to help them and hence
began the missionary exertions of some of my brethren."*

The first minister for the new chapel was a Mr. Earle and he was
responsible for an increase in church membership, but this suffered a
decrease again after he left in 1816. There was however a daily school
for children begun in 1819, and a Sunday School which had 18
members by 1833. Speaking at the 60th anniversary of the chapel in
1868, the then minister, Mr. Poole, described the situation as he had
found it in 1848 when he first preached there. The chapel, he said, was
in a wretched, dilapidated condition and the congregation had dwindled
to 35. There was still, after nearly forty years, a debt of £250 outstanding and he contrasted that situation with the chapel's present condition.
Mr. Poole, "... had been invited to preach for two Sabbaths and they had
stretched away into 25 years." He believed there was not a house in the
village into which he had not entered, and he had always found a hearty
welcome. He referred to the kindness and sympathy he had received in
Hornsea and then said while he was pastor here Skipsea was united
with Hornsea and he calculated that in his journeying between the two
places, in all kinds of weather, he had travelled no less than 20,000
miles. During his residence here he had preached for every
denomination but one; and it was not his fault that he had not preached
for the Episcopalians in their noble old building.

In 1868 the chapel originally built for 250 was becoming too small
owing to the influx of new residents and visitors brought by train, and
new premises would be needed. There were now over 120 people in the
church fellowship. Mr. Poole pointed out that Mr. Joseph Wade was
selling land at six shillings a yard and he thought it advisable to enquire
about the possibility of building a new chapel. Land was in fact later
bought at the junction of New Road and what was then called Cliff Lane
from Mr. Wade, who generously reduced the price from £390 to £290.
Two years later Mr. Bainton of Arram Hall paid for the building of the
manse, next to the site of the future church. A committee set up in 1870

was able to raise £2,200 of the £2,600 needed for the new church by 1874. The church was built mainly by local tradesmen, Messrs. Hulse and Stephenson, bricklayers and plasterers, H. and W. Barr, joiners, and James Barr, plumber and glazier. The clock tower of the church had the bricks raised for building by means of a horse working a rope and pulley. As the clock tower rose in height the horse had to walk almost as far as Westbourne Road to get the bricks up to the top.

The opening service of the new church was held in July 1874 and is described, of course, in the Hornsea Gazette. The preacher that day was the Reverend Enoch Mellor and his text was taken from Matthew 27, "And behold the veil of the temple was rent in twain from the top to the bottom." The Gazette describes the subsequent events very graphically:-

"An eloquent and powerful sermon was preached by the Rev. Mellor but as he expounded on this text, a storm that had been threatening for some little time, burst over the town, the lightning which was very vivid, lighting up the whole building and being succeeded by loud peals of thunder, to the evident alarm and disquietude of several in the congregation. Dr. Mellor however continued his discourse and in the midst of the awful storm, his undaunted bearing allayed in no small degree the fears of those who were listening to him."

After the inaugural service came a celebratory meal but it seemed that the weather had not yet finished with the attempts of the church members to make this a day to remember. As the Gazette records:-

"On adjourning to the tents to partake of a cold collation it was found that the rain had penetrated through the canvas and done serious mischief to the viands. While the friends were partaking of the good things provided for them, the rain again fell very heavily and it was found necessary to resort to the protection of umbrellas which of course prevented the full enjoyment of this part of the proceedings, but the utmost good humour prevailed."

The new Church could seat 500 people and the final £400 of the cost of building the church was promised by donors on the opening day. This was a very fine achievement and one of which church members were rightly proud.

The Wesleyan Methodists

The beginning of the Industrial Revolution saw a marked increase in the population of England and the development of the large industrial towns. The Established Church was still working in the pattern of the old agricultural villages and market towns of the pre-industrial era, and was slow to respond to the new needs. A group of earnest young clerics at Oxford, who, by their strict rules of conduct and their methodical way of performing their religious duties, had earned for themselves the name of Methodists tried by means of open air meetings to bring Christianity to the people. This movement under the leadership of John Wesley became, by the middle of the 18th century, an independent church.

In Hornsea at that time the Established Church was going through a period of declining influence. From 1721 to 1831 there was no resident Vicar in Hornsea, and the parish was under the charge of a curate. The church building which was damaged during the hurricane of 1732 was not completely repaired until the restoration of 1868, so that too was in a sorry state.

Into this situation came the first mission from the Methodists of Hull. There seem to have been no records kept of the missions sent out to the villages of Holderness, but sometime between 1770 and 1780 a group of Methodists was formed in Hornsea. As most of the new converts were cottagers with very little money to spare, the first meeting place for the group was in a room at Low Hall in Southgate, which from 1777 was an inn. Later the group had the use of a granary near the inn, and the meetings were held by the light of hurricane lamps in the winter. In an account of the development of Methodism in Hornsea written by R. A. Loten is a description of that early time. "The evangelists encountered little or nothing of violent opposition: the people incased in prejudice and indifference simply left them severely alone."

Certainly by 1798 when the Reverend George Lambert, minister of the Fish Street Independent Chapel in Hull, visited Hornsea, to undergo a course of sea bathing, he found only a small number of Methodists who had by that time a room fitted up for a meeting place. To his surprise it was an elderly woman who conducted the service.

Hornsea was eventually included in the Patrington Methodist Circuit which encompassed 40 villages altogether, but, because of the distance from Patrington, visits from the minister were few and far between and it was found that converts were drawn away to other services. In these circumstances it was an act of faith for the Hornsea Methodists to build a chapel capable of holding 250 people in 1814 on land at the corner of Back Southgate and Chambers Lane.

The following years must have been financially difficult ones for the new chapel in the depression which followed the end of the French Revolutionary and Napoleonic Wars. The Patrington circuit figures show a drop in the collections from £47 in 1815 for example, to £18 in 1816.

The year 1834 saw a great revival in enthusiasm in the Methodist Church throughout the country and Holderness was no exception. It was found possible to take a third minister onto the Patrington Circuit and to form a new circuit centred on Hornsea. This circuit had Atwick, Bewholme, Brandesburton and Skirlaugh amongst the 20 villages gathered into it. By this time there were 60 members of the Hornsea Chapel and the new circuit had two ministers to serve it. It is interesting to read the details of the senior minister's accounts at this time which were as follows:-

Board	£7	1s	0
Quarterage	£8	8s	0
Washing	£1	1s	0
Servant	£2	0	0
Candles		6s	10d
Shoeing & farrier		18s	8d
Horse Bill		7s	6d
Horse Rent	£1	12s	6d
Coach		4s	0

With the increase in income over the next twenty years the stipend of the senior minister was raised by 1854 to £100 a year; the junior minister received £45 a year.

To augment the services of the two ministers there were several local preachers, each affectionately known by his idiosyncrasies. The barber Benjamin West, who lived in one of the four cottages in the churchyard which were pulled down in 1898, was a very colourful character with four special sermons. One was for the springtime on, "The singing of the birds." One for the summer, "Is there no balm in Gilead?" For autumn the theme was, "We all do fare as leaf," and for the winter, "The Harvest is past." Another local tradesman was not so well organised in his preaching; he used to say, "I've two sermons in my head but they're so mixed I can't separate them so you're bound to hear them together.".

Over the years Chapel membership rose as did the Sunday School membership. The Sunday School was held in a long narrow schoolroom which had a little black stove at one end. Begun in 1829 with 36 children there were 43 children by 1854 on the books. The Methodists had also organised a weekday school from 1829 until the opening of the National School in 1845. After the railway was opened in 1864 the population of the town nearly doubled and all the chapels felt a need for new premises. Land was bought in Newbegin for the building of Trinity Chapel and this was opened on June 30th 1870. After the opening service a public tea was served for 750 people in the nearby Public Rooms. Such a large number had to be served at three sittings.

The new chapel could seat 600 people compared to the old one which could only seat 250; the schoolrooms could accommodate a much bigger Sunday School too, and by the time of the Sunday School Jubilee in 1896 there were 120 children on the register being taught by 29 teachers.

The Primitive Methodists

At the beginning of the 19th century a schism occurred in the Methodist Church. The new movement originated around the Pottery Towns and centred on Tunstall. The emphasis of the services was to be on praying and singing with only short sermons and the chief attraction was the holding of open air services or camp meetings. The leader of the movement, Hugh Bourne, was expelled from the Methodist Society and with William Clowes formed in 1811 the Primitive Methodist Connexion with some 200 members initially. In 1819 Clowes came on a mission to Hull and helped to start the fourth circuit of the new church having some 24 preaching places. The next year the first Conference was held in Hull. The tide of evangelism rose to its height in the 1830's and left behind in many of the small villages not one, but two Methodist chapels - Aldbrough, Atwick, Hatfield, Leven, Bewholme, Catwick, Beeford, Seaton, Riston, Brandesburton, Brandesburton Moortown, Mappleton and Cowden all had Wesleyan and Primitive chapels. However small the community so deeply held was the feeling of differentiation that all obstacles could be overcome to achieve the building of the chapel. At Atwick the Primitive Methodist chapel was built from cobbles gathered by men and women of the congregation from the beach.

In Hornsea the first Primitive chapel was built in 1835 on the site of Melbourne House, Westgate, with the Ministers house called Clowes Cottage in Back Westgate on the site of the house now called Coningsby.

The Market Place chapel to seat 400 was built in 1864 at a cost of £1,000 and afterwards the old chapel in Westgate was pulled down and a new manse for the minister was built on the site.

This old building in Newbegin is believed to have been John Scaife's cottage, where the original Independent group held their first services around 1800.

Hornsea as a Spa

The custom of drinking spring water for medicinal purposes goes back to Roman times. In England "taking the waters" became very popular at the beginning of the 18th century. The enthusiasm for imbibing quantities of mineral spring water was followed a few years later by the cult of sea bathing for curing various ailments. Scarborough, having already achieved popularity as a Spa in the 17th century by means of two springs, a "chalybeate" and a "saline" spring, was one of the pioneers of sea bathing, and as early as 1730 had many visitors for that purpose. Naturally other seaside towns were quick to follow the example of Scarborough since "taking the cure" was responsible for bringing to a town many well-to-do people with money to spend. Both Bridlington and Hornsea discovered "chalybeate springs," that is water with dissolved minerals giving a tart flavour, and began to attract visitors. Hornsea had in fact three surface springs; one near the site of the Marine Hotel, one near the future Bewholme Lane, and a third which rose between Westgate and the Mere. The latter was the "chalybeate spring" which was developed as a spa and was indicated on a map of 1778 drawn by R. Pele showing "Hornsea Meer" with the note added, "at the North East end is a spring of Victriolic quality nearly as strong as Scarborough Spaw." This spring rose in a small enclosure between Westgate and the Mere which was owned by a Stephen Linskin according to the Reverend W. Smith of Catwick. A shallow well for the convenience of visitors taking the cure was dug out some four feet square and three feet deep with a channel of brick for the overflow to the Mere a few yards away. The well was originally open to the sky but later a brick shelter was built. In attendance during the season was an elderly lady who, with a tin cup attached to a wooden handle, ladled the water out of the well. She then filled a horn drinking cup and handed it to the "clergy, nobility and gentry" who after paying her a trifle took their prescribed dose.

A brick shelter which was built later was eight feet square, thus allowing a two foot wide brick surround to the well. The walls had openings for windows as well as a doorway. Mr. Linskin sold his enclosure sometime after 1825 to Mr. Constable of Wassand who let it to a local character known as "Bacca Billy" from his habit of smoking an ounce of tobacco every day. Billy and his wife lived in a cottage nearby and kept the garden around the well gay with flowers. A small charge was made for entering the garden and drinking the water; and the well was still in existence around 1870. After that date the well was filled in and the enclosure used as a vegetable garden until after 1928.

There seem to be two possible sites for this spring, one in Westgate opposite the Infants School, and the other on the Mereside to the west of the old peoples' bungalows. Stephen Linskin was awarded a narrow strip of common land there in 1809, and on the 1854 map there seems to be another strip with a cottage on it which could have been Bacca Billy's. There was, however, a spring rising at the back of "The Pillars" which empties into the Mere alongside Grebe House and there was a small triangular enclosure on Westgate alongside the stream which was not built on until after 1928.

By the end of the 18th century the custom of visitors from Hull and other towns staying at Hornsea in order to try the effects of sea bathing on their health was well established, as witness the visit of the Reverend George Lambert in 1798. The summer visitors had to obtain lodgings in the small cottages in the town or else try to find accommodation at one of the four hotels which were at that time little better than ale houses. Two of the Hotels were in the Market Place; these were the New Hotel, and the Prince of Wales. The third hotel was the Old Hotel in Southgate, formerly known as Low Hall, and the fourth was called the Hare and Hounds. Until the influx of summer visitors began these inns would be used only for the stabling of the carts and traps of the farmers on market day, and providing food and drink for country folk. The arrival of the carriages and servants of the gentry and their more exacting requirements for food and accommodation would bring many changes in the quiet country town.

The journey from Hull over the poor roads of Holderness lasted over three hours, and travel was limited to the drier months of the year. A turnpike road had been built from Hull to Flinton in 1767 and this would provide a reasonably good surface for that part of the journey. The roads in the coastal area were very bad indeed. Writing in October 1777 the Reverend Dade noted that, "... in a month's time Aldboro will be inaccessible to Barmston on account of the Road." By 1821 a coach service was running daily to Hull and this was supplemented in the summer months by Messrs. Wardell and Chaffer from 1829 onwards. An advertisement in the Hull Packet and East Riding Times of June 1830 gives details of this service:-

"Messrs. Wardell and Chaffer return their most sincere thanks for the liberal support given to their Hornsea Coach during the last season and respectfully Inform the Public that they commence running their Union Coach on Monday, June 14th from their office, Land of Green Ginger, at 8 in the morning."

One of the entertainments in the summer for the visitors were the races held on the sands of Hornsea Beck between the 17th and 24th July. The races were followed in the evening by a ball which might have been held in the assembly room mentioned in the Manor Court Rolls in

Newbegin in 1811.

Hornsea had altered little in character from the small country town it had been for generations past. With a population of only 790 it had, as shown by the 1821 directory, the usual village tradesmen - blacksmith, shoemaker, bricklayer, butcher and tallow chandler, grocers and drapers, tailors, wheelwrights, saddlers, clock maker, weaver, hairdresser and miller. The only slight indication of any change comes in the presence of two surgeons and a druggist, who might have been attracted to a town where rich invalids congregated for some weeks every year, and also in the lapidary who polished and mounted stones for brooches, necklaces, etc.

In 1831 there were still only four lodging houses available for the accommodation of visitors. It was not until 1837 and the opening of the first Marine Hotel that the town's role as a seaside resort led to any changes in its appearance. This building on the edge of the cliff, exposed to all the winds, was isolated from the cottages and small shops of the town which were gathered together around the church. A record of the opening of this Hotel is in the Hull Advertiser for June 1837:-

> "The growing importance of this Watering Place had induced Daniel Jameson to open an Establishment called the Marine Hotel - Good stabling and coach house."

Also in the Advertiser is an account of the town's festivities on the proclamation of Queen Victoria at the end of that same June, which gives a picture of the place and the people then.

> "June 30th. Her Majesty the Queen was proclaimed at this place on Wednesday last. On the arrival of the writ it was determined that the proceedings should be conducted in a manner worthy the joyous occasion. A subscription was entered into and a procession arranged consisting of the principal inhabitants and visitors, the men on the preventive service, a band of music, flags, etc. The proclamation of Her Majesty was made by W. B. Denton, Esq., who most creditably took a leading part in the proceedings of the day. As Hornsea is now very full of fashionable company, the presence of the ladies who graced the windows added much to the gaiety of the scene. After the procession, the preventive men (Customs Officers), band, flagbearers and others employed were regaled at Strakers Hotel (New Hotel). Other convivial parties were held and long life to Victoria toasted with every demonstration of affectionate loyalty."

That year two coaches a day, the Pilot in the morning and the Union in the afternoon, were run from Hull; these four-in-hand coaches were stabled at the New Hotel and the Victoria, (the new name for the Prince of Wales Hotel.) By 1840 there were 28 lodging houses available, one of which advertised proudly the possession of a bath. The first establishment of the Penny Post in Hornsea was on January 5th 1840. Previously the post had been delivered by means of William Burn, foot postman, who used to set out for Leven at 9 a.m. and return at 1 p.m. From 1840 until 1860 the mail came by mail coach from Hull, arriving at 8.30 a.m. and returning there at 2 p.m. An 1840 directory gives another picture of the town at that time; it describes Hornsea as being:-

"... a small but pleasant town and bathing place which since 1831 has been considerably improved and enlarged owing to its popularity as a bathing place. The town is sheltered by rising grounds on the north and south and consists chiefly of four straggling streets branching from the Market Place which has the shaft of an ancient cross elevated on several steps."

The pleasures of the place were given as, "... fairs held on August 13th and December 17th, the first for pleasure and pedlary and the last for cattle, and races held in July on the long stretches of sand, arising from the lost villages of Hide and Hornsea Beck now buried in the sands, which rise by a very gradual ascent and are left bare for a considerable distance at low water." These races were responsible for bringing less desirable visitors to the town on occasion. In 1834 a police constable from Hull and the Hornsea constable apprehended at the races a juvenile gang of pickpockets who were dressed in smock frocks. One of the boys had on him three silk handkerchiefs and the magistrate, Mr. Bethell, sent all the boys to the House of Correction.

The population had increased to 1,000 by 1841 and to cater for the seasonal invasion of fashion-conscious young ladies there were four milliners and three straw hat makers.

One of the most important new residents at that time was a member of a large Hull timber firm who is listed, because of his connections with trade, among the gentry of the town, but as "John Wade, Esquire." In 1846 he built Hornsea House in Eastgate, a, "...neat mansion," as it was described in Whites Directory of that year. This large house stood for 100 years on the site of what is now Hornsea School. All that remains of it today are the fine specimen trees in the grounds of the school, and the two lodges, now 11 and 17 Eastgate, built at the two entrances.

By 1846 the growing number of visitors to the town led to an increase in lodging houses to 67, and also to the enlargement of the Marine Hotel to provide nearly 200 bedrooms. The resort was still attracting the more well-to-do visitors as can be seen from the prices quoted in an advertisement in June 1845 for the Marine Hotel. It should be remembered that the prices are not for the peak summer months.

"This establishment is now open for the reception of Families. Terms for the months of May, June, October and November, Two guineas per week, including Board, Sitting and Bed Room.

Children 7 shillings - 10 shillings Male Servants 21 shillings
Female Servants 18 shillings
Warm and Shower Baths, Billiards, Superior Stabling
Lock up, Coach Houses etc., on the Premises.

As well as enlarging the accommodation a refreshment pavilion was built on the sands and a subterranean passage through the cliffs connected this to the hotel.

Of the, "several houses lately built in the town and on the sea shore for visitors," as the 1846 Directory puts it, two groups can be identified. One group, then called Marine Terrace, is now known as 1 to 3 Marine Drive. Some 50 yards in front of Marine Terrace, at a comfortable distance then from the beach, was a Coast Guard Station built in 1830, with a flagstaff for signalling in front of the station. The other group was Swiss Terrace in Newbegin, with Marine Villa next door, built at what was then the very outskirts of the town.

The bricks for all this building were produced locally. The brickyard in Westgate had closed by 1800, but there were other brick and tile makers including a Richard Lamplugh in Hornsea Burton. It is his brickyard which is mentioned by Bedell in this charming passage from his book, "An Account of Hornsea":-

"A fragment now about 150 yards long of an ancient lane once leading from Rowlston Field through Hornsea Burton, towards Hornsea Beck might be mentioned as a sort of sentimental antiquity which will hardly survive another half century. The southern end of it has been cut off from Rowlston Field within the last three or four years by a brickyard. It runs obliquely to the cliff, where of course it is continually wasting and points now only towards a waste of water. On the east side of it there is a bank and ditch with a few wind-beaten stunted thorns etc. Before the sward which had overgrown it was cut up with carting, this was a pleasant spot in the spring full of cowslips, and suggestive of reflections on the oblivion to which man and his works hasten."

The importance of the town as a seaside resort was steadily growing. The number of bathing machines increased from two or three in 1807 to about twenty by 1846. Visitors could also take a trip out to sea in the one boat available. There was no deep sea fishing; all sea fish was brought into the town from Skipsea although shrimping took place on the shore. Apart from shrimping and the sedate sea bathing from bathing machines, there were only donkey rides along the beach to entertain visitors. Apart from a small number of weekly newspapers brought out from Hull by coach some reading matter was at first available from a Religious Free Library at what is now 8 Market Place, supervised by the postmaster William Henderson. This was later supplemented by a Hornsea Reading Society which started in 1843 and had after 4 years a library of about 200 books. The 30 members of the

Society paid a penny a week and no doubt visitors would be able to borrow books too. The growing number of ailing visitors was by this time able to provide a living for 4 surgeons. One of the visitors to the small select seaside resort which Hornsea had become by mid-century was Charlotte Bronte, the novelist. At the end of September 1853, according to Mrs. Gaskell's "Life of Charlotte Bronte," she came to spend a week with her friend Miss Wooler who was staying in lodgings at what was then part of Swiss Terrace and is now 94 Newbegin.

In the surrounding countryside the traditional sports were still actively pursued. The Holderness foxhounds hunted twice a week in the winter and met at Wassand Hall, Rise Mill and Owstwick. Sir Clifford Constable ran a pack of staghounds from Burton Constable and meets were arranged at Ellerby Mill, Sproatley and Coniston. One enthusiast for this sporting life was the Hornsea postmaster, in 1858 a Thomas Straker, who in the directory of that year was described as post master and trainer and dealer in all kinds of sporting dogs. Farmers and businessmen still travelled by horseback and were occasionally robbed by highwaymen. Mr. J. A. Wade, who inherited Hornsea House in 1853, was said to have been robbed of his purse and watch and chain when travelling into Hull on horseback. In 1855 a presentation was made by gentlemen and farmers of North Holderness to a police superintendent of Leven as a token of gratitude for the apprehension of highway robbers and breaking up of gangs of robbers. Interest in outdoor sports meant that the Hornsea Races were still a popular event and were to continue so until 1885. The races of 1857 as described in the Hull Packet and East Riding Times had an added attraction to amuse the visitors:-

"On Monday this village presented a most lively appearance, it being the day on which the races are generally held there. The Sax horn Band from Brandesburton came into the town in the morning and paraded the principal streets, charming the visitors and inhabitants with their sweet harmony, after which they went down to the sea side and onto the sea in a boat which gave a very fine effect."

A brass band was first formed in Hornsea in 1856 when some members of the church choir gave an instrumental concert in the National School, together with songs from members of the Sigglesthorne Vocal Society. This concert was so successful that a committee was formed by the vicar to raise funds to buy more instruments. This brass band was to perform three evenings a week on the sands near the coastguard station during the season, and some years later a bandstand was built there. Although Hornsea was popular as a seaside resort with the more well-to-do, the town was still inaccessible to the poorer section of the community. Undoubtedly the building of the Hull to Hornsea railway was to change the town from a select, genteel watering place to something much more popular.

16 School Time

From the parish registers which date from 1654, it would seem that some form of schooling was available in Hornsea in the 17th century for three out of the four churchwardens of the day could sign their names. The first record of any resident teacher in the town is in an entry in the Manor Court Rolls for 1698 when a, "Thomas Harrison of hornsea Skool Maister," is mentioned. The register records the deaths of two school masters in the 18th century, namely Alexander Stirks who died in 1743 and William Brown who died in 1768. In the Manor Court Rolls in 1800 is an entry referring to a John Hodgson, schoolmaster.

Throughout England the teaching of reading and writing on Sundays in Sunday Schools was begun in 1780 and these schools were often held in the vestry of the church or at the foot of the bell tower, and this may have been the case in Hornsea.

A report by the Government Inspector for schools in 1818 gives details of the schools in Hornsea with Hornsea Burton, (population 704.) The report says that there were no endowments for scholars although Richard Bethell, Esq., the Lord of the Manor, gave 10 guineas per annum for the education of 10 children and there were 45 pupils in the school. There were also at the same time two dame schools for children under eight years of age, one with 27 children the other with 21. The Inspector commented that,

"There are very few in the parish who are not capable of paying for the instruction of their own children, nor are the poorer classes desirous of their own children availing themselves of the opportunities they possess."

From the East Riding directory of 1821 it appears that there were two teachers in Hornsea then, a George Brown and a John Nicholson, and the school is described as a Church School. By 1833 there were four Sunday Schools in Hornsea all supported by voluntary contributions according to an, "Address to the House of Commons," that year. Two of these schools were Anglican with 70 scholars, while the Independent Chapel had 18 Sunday Scholars, and the Wesleyan Methodists had 36. Both of the last two schools had lending libraries attached. During the week there were five schools attended by 121 children, all of whose parents paid for their schooling. Two of these schools were for dissenters - one for 15 pupils was opened in 1819, and the other with 24 pupils had begun in 1829.

Another important event in the history of education in England was the creation of a National Society in 1811 by Dr. Bell. This society was responsible for building many schools throughout the country. The members, predominantly Anglican, were anxious to educate the children in the Christian tradition and great importance was attached to a close connection with the church. A Diocesan Inspector visited the schools regularly and examined the children on their knowledge of Scripture, of the Catechism and the Prayer Book. Other subjects were under the scrutiny of Her Majesty's Inspectors. Geography, Arithmetic, Spelling and "Tables" were all taught, and there was an emphasis on, "... plenty of sewing for the girls."

In 1845 a National School was opened on the Mereside in Hornsea on land given by the Reverend Charles Constable of Wassand. The school had accommodation for 200 children and cost £3650 to build. The money was raised by public subscription, together with a grant from the National Society. That same year an Infants' School, the building of which was paid for by Mary, Lady Strickland, (who was the Reverend Constable's daughter,) opened in Westgate. This school had accommodation for 65 children and was the last cobble building to be built in Hornsea. It remained as an Infants school until 1935.

To help pay for their instruction at the National School the children brought a weekly fee of two pence known as the "School Pence."

In 1851 one of Her Majesty's Inspectors visited the Mereside School and noted in his report, "A village school in the purely agricultural district of the East Riding where education was much neglected till lately. There are not so many children in attendance as might fairly be expected from the size of the place." Since education did not become compulsory until 1891 many of the poorer parents would consider it more important to have their children out at work than wasting their time in school. Children were still expected to work hard and long and the parish register records the deaths of three ten year old boys immediately prior to 1811. All three were killed at harvest time by wagons running over them. Girls were still regarded as inferior in understanding and the Inspector found the Hornsea girls had very little opportunity to get an education. The 34 girls had only an untrained teacher to take them and were, "... in a low state as to instruction, not at present learning the usual subjects and little advanced in arithmetic." The 36 boys did at least have a trained master to supervise them although equipment was limited. They were segregated from the girls and sat on loose benches at two rows of desks. There were three blackboards but only a moderate supply of books and maps. All the children, according to the report, were clean and neat, and discipline was fair. After the passing the Education Act grants were made by the Government towards the cost of the National Schools but the children still continued to bring their weekly pennies and the Church and the National Society still contributed, as can be seen from the accounts for the Mereside School in 1879.

Balance in Hand	15- 1-6	Salaries of Teachers	199-16- 6
Government Grant	91-12-0	Books and Stationery	7- 6-11
Subscription	47- 5-0	Fuel and Light	7- 8- 7
Society Subscription	3-12-0	Furniture and Cleaning	19- 8- 2
Collections in Church	20- 4-1	Insurance	9- 6
School Pence	62-10-6	Other Expenses	9- 0
		Balance	4-16- 5
	£ 240- 5-1		£240- 5- 1

A School Board with five members, being people of standing in the community, was formed in 1884 and responsibility for running the school passed to this Board.

As well as the state schools, there were several private schools in Hornsea in the 19th century. The numbers increased until in 1858 there were seven. One of these, the Holderness Boarding Academy, was on Fair Place across from the National School. The headmaster of this academy for, "Young Gentlemen as Boarders and Day Pupils," Mr. Thomas Smith, is described in P. Loten's account given elsewhere. A typical prospectus of the time gives the course of study as, "... comprising Instruction in the Holy Scripture, the Classics and Mathematics, the English and Modern Languages critically with composition in each and Elocution, Ancient and Modern History, Geography with Mapping, the use of the Globe, Natural Philosophy with lessons on objects, Natural History, Arithmetic and Writing."

Towards the last half of the 19th century the realization of the importance of physical fitness led to an emphasis on drill and organized team games. The syllabus for Brampton House School in Railway Street speaks of, "Summer bathing under careful supervision," and of the boys being drilled regularly by a qualified instructor. Mention is made of the Cricket and Football field, and anxious parents were assured that the, "Drainage and Sanitation are certified as being in the best possible order."

Another well known private school was St. Bedes, Atwick Road. An account by Dr. H. I. Loten of school life there at the turn of the 19th and 20th centuries is given elsewhere.

By the time of Queen Victoria's Golden Jubilee in 1887 there were some 250 school children at the Board School and dames' schools in the town, who were given tea followed by sports to mark the occasion.

Joseph Armytage Wade (1817-1896)
by Mike Sewell

The most important personality in Hornsea from the 1860's to the 1890's was Joseph Armytage Wade, who dominated the life of the town to such an extent that he was nicknamed, "The King of Hornsea."

His family background was in the timber importing business and his grandfather had founded the firm of Richard Wade, Sons and Company in Hull at the end of the 18th century. Wade and his younger brother, John, inherited the company jointly in 1853 and at the same time Wade was bequeathed Hornsea House and associated land. This was as the result of the deaths within a short time of Wade's uncle, John Wade, (who built the house,) and also his elder brother and his father.

For almost ten years Wade had no impact upon Hornsea, except to extend Hornsea House in order to accommodate his family. Then, from 1862, Wade's various activities began to have an increasing effect upon the economic and social life of the town.

Wade's first great scheme was to promote and build a railway line from Hull to Hornsea. (See Chapter 18 below.) Although the Hull and Hornsea Railway Company did not survive long as an independent concern, it did transform the nature of the town. Hull could now be reached in 40 minutes, which led to Hornsea becoming a dormitory town. This caused a surge in building, in which Wade was involved, both as a speculator in land and also through the activities of his Hornsea Brick and Tile Company which was located on the site of the present Hornsea Freeport. The company's most famous products were the Patent Interlocking Roofing Tiles, or "Acorn Tiles," as they are better known. These were developed in collaboration with John Cherry, who was Wade's works manager. They also worked together when Wade founded the Hydraulic Engineering Works adjacent to the brick and tile works. This company manufactured water pumps which created a lively export trade and were also used in the building of the Manchester Ship Canal.

Wade's enterprises provided much employment for the people of Hornsea and the town expanded as the result of the arrival of the railway. The Grosvenor Estate, (Burton, Eastbourne and Wilton Roads,) the Lansdowne Estate, (Cliff Road, Hartley Street and Esplanade,) and also New Road, Railway Street and Wilton Terrace all grew up in the years immediately after the railway opened in 1864.

In the same year Wade founded the Hornsea Gas, Light and Coke Company with a gasworks on Hull Road. Gas was provided both for private houses and also street lamps. (There was also a shorter-lived gasworks in Hartley Street.)

The arrival of the railway also caused Hornsea to become a regionally important seaside resort which catered mostly for middle class visitors, although working class "excursionists" were more prominent after the Bank Holiday Act of 1871. Many Hornsea people turned their hand to providing lodgings for visitors. Joseph Wade recognised the potential for profit and founded the Hornsea Pier Company in 1866. (See Chapter 19 below.)

In addition to his commercial activities, Wade was heavily involved in the public life of the town. This stemmed mainly from his chairmanship of the Hornsea Local Board of Health, from its foundation in 1864. He served until 1889, (except for one year,) and under his leadership, by 1874 the town was provided with a deep drainage and sewerage system, with a sea outfall, which, although crude by today's standards, was much superior to the cess pits and open sewers which had been prevalent before. In 1878 a new waterworks was opened on Atwick Road, from where the town was provided with clean water from a borehole.

From 1872 to 1883 Wade was elected as one of the People's Churchwardens of the parish church. During these years he came into frequent conflict with the Reverend Edmund Tew, particularly over the provision and location of a new cemetery. Wade prevailed and the cemetery opened on Southgate in 1885 under the auspices of the Local Board of Health.

Wade was also committed to social and philanthropic work, both in Hull and Hornsea. In Hull he was one of the founders of the Hull Working Men's Club and also the Temporary Home for Recently Fallen Women. He also paid for poor children from the Hull Ragged Schools and the Industrial Schools to come by train to Hornsea and have a day out in the fresh seaside air. Wade was also the chairman of the trustees of the Hull, East Riding and Lincolnshire Institute for the Deaf and Dumb and he paid for the inmates and workers to have an annual outing to Hornsea.

In Hornsea it was said that he was always the first to give relief if sickness overtook a poor man's family and he only had to hear of a needy case and relief was immediately provided. As the result of these charitable activities, Wade was known as, "The Poor Man's Friend."

Wade was connected with the foundation of the Hornsea Tennis and Cricket Club and allowed them to play on land which he owned near Hornsea Bridge station. He was also the main patron of the Hornsea Horticultural Society and its annual show was held in the grounds of Hornsea House. Other organisations patronised by Wade included the Hornsea Young Men's Association and, being a strict teetotaller, the Church of England Temperance Society.

In politics Wade was a Liberal and, although not standing for political office himself, he supported Liberal candidates at both local and national level. He helped to found the Hornsea and District Liberal Club in 1880 and acquired the old Wesleyan Methodist chapel in Back Southgate for their premises.

Despite being held in great affection by the poor and underprivileged, Wade was not well-regarded by some of the people from his own social background. This stemmed from his somewhat disagreeable character when confronted with dissent or argument and he could be very rude to those whom he felt were not of his way of thinking. He was not the sort of man who could be persuaded to change his mind. This led to estrangement from other "worthies" who were involved in public life and, although Wade supported such good causes as the lifeboat, he was not directly involved because of disagreements. He adopted a proprietorial air towards his own activities in Hornsea. This caused resentment and there were several attempts by the Hornsea Ratepayers Association and the "New Party" to oust him from the Local Board of Health. This finally happened in 1889, when it was felt that some younger blood was needed and that Wade had been in office for so long that he could no longer distinguish between his public activities and his commercial schemes.

Joseph Armytage Wade died on 3rd March 1896, aged 78, at his home and, despite his unpopularity in some quarters, his funeral was reputedly the largest ever to occur in Hornsea. A special train brought representatives from local government and the Hull commercial and industrial community and they joined with local people to pay their last respects to, "The King of Hornsea."

18 The Hull to Hornsea Railway

A railway for Hornsea was first considered in 1846 by the York and North Midland Railway Company, chairman George Hudson, the so-called Railway King. The line was to be part of the Hull and Selby Railway and the Hornsea works were to begin in 1847. A branch line to Hornsea from the Hull to Bridlington line was to start at Leconfield and the terminal station was to be on Atwick Road near to the windmill. However, George Hudson was ruined by over-ambitious speculation and the scheme came to nothing.

It was not until 1862 that Joseph Armytage Wade formed a company to build a railway from Hull to Hornsea. Wade had inherited Hornsea House in 1853 and played a leading role in Hornsea life for the next 40 years. The railway was his first enterprise in Hornsea. The second was the formation of the Brick and Tile Works and the third was the ill-fated Hornsea Pier.

A Railway Bill was introduced into Parliament for the new company by Lord Hotham in 1862, the subscribers J.A. Wade, William Wright, Benjamin Haworth, Thomas Sykes, Edward Broosheft, Samuel Egginton and Thomas Haller. The company had a capital of £10,000 and the railway was to be completed within 5 years of the passing of the Act. The rates to be charged for passengers were:-

1st Class..........................3d a mile
2nd Class.........................2d a mile
3rd Class.........................1½d a mile

In the summer of 1862 a procession of local personages, preceded by the Hornsea Brass Band marched from Hornsea House to what is now Bank Terrace in Southgate. Here, watched all the school children of the town, the ceremony of turning the first sod was performed by Mr. Wade. To mark the occasion Mr. Wade had been given a commemorative spade and wheel barrow by the Board of Directors. The barrow was of Italian walnut carved to represent a rhinoceros. The head and legs were polished but the body was carved to imitate the skin of the animal. (A rhinoceros had been chosen since this was the Wade family crest.)

The building of the railway presented some difficulties. The clay soil of the Holderness plain was unsuitable for building the necessary embankments so that large quantities of ballast had to be fetched from Kelsey Hill. The line was originally to have finished at Hornsea Bridge Station. The extension, built over the boggy land between Hornsea

Bridge and the terminus involved the construction of a wooden viaduct with expensive piles to support the line, ranging from a depth of 2 feet near the Mere to 15 feet at the terminus.

Another difficulty was the unreliability of the labour force. The famous navigators, or "navvies," of the day, who provided the labour for the building of the canals, railways, bridges and tunnels of the era received comparatively large wages, about £2. 10 shillings a week, as against the 8 shillings a week of a farm labourer. Although they worked hard for the money, as soon as they received their wages they would go to the nearest public house and drink until their money was gone. In some cases they were drunk from Saturday to Wednesday and would never do a stroke of work until they were penniless and had to. Often the navvies were fined for drunkenness at the local Magistrates' court. At one court in October 1863 a number of half drunken navvies and their friends were so noisy that the Magistrate read the Riot Act to them. Thanks to this habitual drunkenness the contractors were two months overdue with the completion of the railway.

The foundation stone of the terminal station was laid in October 1863 by Richard Wade, the 14 year old eldest son of J. A. Wade, and the line was opened for traffic on March 28th 1864. The estimate for building the line had been £68,000 but the actual cost was nearly double, at £122,000. An account of the opening of the completed line comes from the Hull Packet:-

"The long wished for day has at length arrived. The Hull and Hornsea railway is now open to the public. On Wednesday last the first train started from the Wilmington Station - the arrangements to run from Paragon Street, as we have already stated, being not yet completed, at noon and was well filled with passengers, despite the miserable weather which prevailed. The station and every spot adjacent, was crowded with spectators anxious to witness the departure of the train and as it moved slowly away they cheered lustily. A band inside one of the fore carriages played merrily, and everything was indicative of gladness at the completion of an enterprise which will undoubtedly prove very advantageous to several hitherto more progressive towns, to which the absence of railway communication has certainly been detrimental. Everything went smoothly and the train arrived at its destination in safety at one o'clock, amidst the great cheering of the enormous crowd which had gathered together, and which seemed to be the whole population of Hornsea. During its travel it was greeted every now and then with loud cheering which burst from the lungs of small groups of gazers stood by the cottages near the rail. On Mr. Wade, chairman of the company, the other directors, the secretary, engineers, contractors etc. alighting, the applause was loud and prolonged. When the approbation had subsided, Mr. Wade addressed the assembly and declared the Hull and Hornsea Railway to be open (loud applause and firing) He hoped that it might be the means of affording to hundreds of thousands of people that means of recreation and enjoyment which it placed within their reach, (cheers.) He had the greatest faith in the success of the line. Mr. Wade concluded by asking the crowd to give his brother directors, the engineer and the secretary, and others who had worked zealously, three hearty cheers. This request having been duly complied with, a procession headed by the band, walked to the chairman's house. The town was profusely adorned with flags, banners and devices bearing suitable mottoes and everybody seemed to keep the day as a holiday. Evidence of rejoicing were not wanting, neither were good wishes. Mr. Wade fearful that he should not receive enough good wishes wished himself one. In a transparency exhibited directly over the front entrance of Mr. Wade's house was the following sentence, "Prosperity to the Chairman and Company of the Hull and Hornsea Railway." Several trains ran to and fro during the day, and when the last train arrived at Hornsea no accident of any kind had happened."

The railway was a single line run by the Hull and Hornsea Railway Company using carriages, good wagons and engines leased from the North Eastern Railway Company. From the start, the Hull and Hornsea Railway Company was in financial difficulties. Even though the coming of the railway changed Hornsea for ever, it never came up to its promoters' expectations, neither in passengers, nor in goods traffic and after only two years it was taken over by the North Eastern Railway.

The line was made double track in the early 20th century and a day return to Hull was for many years only one shilling. The first station master appointed was drowned whilst bathing but for twenty-five years from 1875 to 1900 the stationmaster was, very appropriately, a Mr. W. Train. (At the same time Hornsea had a Mr. Smith the blacksmith too!)

Hornsea Town railway station was designed by Rawlins Gould of York, who also designed the York Register Office. After the line closed in 1964 the building became increasingly derelict, but was rescued by local enterprise and has been converted into housing.

19 The Contest of the Hornsea Piers

The first piers were mainly built of stone and served as a protection for a fishing harbour or small port. Later one of the symbols of prosperity and success for a Victorian seaside resort was the building of a pier for promenading, These piers took the form of a very long timber roadway supported on metal piles. Some of these Victorian piers survive on the West and the south coast but most of those built on the north-east coast were wrecked either by the fierce storms of the North Sea or collisions with ships which even in the last quarter of the 19th century were mainly sailing ships and consequently difficult to control in stormy weather.

In Hornsea it was Joseph Wade who in 1866 obtained a Board of Trade order to build a pier; the order to become void if after five years no pier was built. The strength of the current along the Holderness coast and the shifting nature of the sea bed presented difficulties. To gauge the effect of these factors Mr. Wade had ten piles driven into the foreshore a few yards south of the end of New Road. To try to prevent erosion and help to form sand banks a barricade of twigs and hurdles was built along the beach at the same point. Unfortunately an exceptionally high tide combined with a storm flooded the area and destroyed the pile driving engine, leaving the ten piles standing forlornly there, to be christened by local wits, "The Ten Virgins."

Meanwhile another very enterprising businessman, Pierre Henri Martin du Gillon of Sheffield, had bought land in Hornsea Burton and was planning to develop it. As part of this plan he wished to build a pier and dredge out a harbour. In 1874 he came over from Sheffield and after several rebuffs managed to see Mr. Wade in his office at the brickworks. Mr. du Gillon left this interview believing that he had an outline agreement with Mr. Wade to build a road across the latter's land south of the railway station to the foot of his proposed pier, some 818 yards in distance. In this belief he had plans prepared by his surveyor for a sea wall, a promenade and an aquarium as the first stage of his development scheme. The Board of Trade order of 1866 had lapsed after five years, but Mr. Wade renewed his option and formed the Hornsea Pier Company in 1873. Wade's pier was for a site about 100 yards south of the railway station so that from 1874 onwards there were two ambitious, successful men each with a plan for a pier on sites only 700 yards apart.

Conflict was bound to develop since access from the railway station, (which all holiday visitors used,) to du Gillon's pier would be over land owned by his rival pier builder Mr. Wade. The year 1875 saw an ever more acrimonious series of letters pass between the two men until finally in December du Gillon applied for a compulsory purchase order for land owned by Wade as the only means of obtaining public access to his pier site. As chairman of the Local Board of Health, Wade called a special meeting at which he alleged that this land might be essential for the future construction of a town sewer.

Remarks made by Wade which seem only too typical of him were quoted in the Hornsea Gazette. "The position of the Board would receive further misrepresentation in the paper as it perhaps made it sell," and about his rival, du Gillon, he said, "... everyone interested would have to take care that the promoter did not get to their blind side. He would have done so with him, (Mr. Wade,) if he had closed with his first offer." This remark so infuriated du Gillon that he had printed at his own expense a pamphlet called, "An Abridged Version of Hornsea Pier Negotiations," a collection of the correspondence between the two men with some additional comments from du Gillon, including some penetrating remarks about Wade's character. "I did not find it difficult to get on what he elegantly calls his blind side, nothing of the sort; the only difficulty I had to contend with during my wearisome negotiation with him were to find the side on which he is not blind. For the man who cannot even see his own interest or that of a community he has so long kept under his tutelage must be stone blind indeed. Why should Mr. Wade's hand be against every man who is not ready to do him vassalage as his Lord and King. There is no one who begrudges him his position as 'first fiddle' but why drive the humble band to rebel because he will not allow them to play even penny trumpets."

Du Gillon sought for and obtained a Board of Trade order in 1876 to construct a pier, as well as two roads, a tramway and a sea wall. As well as the tramway and road running southwards from the station across Mr. Wade's land close to the cliff edge, there was also to be a road from the railway bridge over Rolston Lane, (now Rolston Road,) to join with the cliffside road at the foot of the pier. The protective sea wall was to stretch from south of the pier to the end of New Road, a distance of half a mile. There were also to be depots, warehouses, sheds, toll houses, custom houses and hydraulic lifts, in fact every equipment for the harbour which was to be dredged out alongside the pier. The tramway would cost approximately £1,800 to build and would take the passengers, (divided into 1st and 2nd class,) from the station platform to the end of the pier. There were to be toll gates on both roads and the rates for landing on the pier were calculated in alphabetical order from Ale, Anchors through Cattle, Chimney pots, Corpses (1 shilling each) to Wood and Yarn. This ambitious plan would take a great deal of money and in fact the Hornsea Pier, Promenade and Improvement Company, as du Gillon's company was known, had a capital of £40,000, an immense sum in those days, and offices were opened in the Public Rooms,

Newbegin in 1876.

Wade's original Hornsea Pier Company had its office in the Market Place and here the Annual General Meetings were held from 1874 onwards with Mr. Wade as chairman.

Du Gillon and his architect drew up plans for a whole new town complete with esplanades and crescents of houses surrounding a new church, all to be built in Hornsea Burton. Copies of this map were printed in the Hornsea Gazette in March 1877 and must have roused a great deal of comment in the small town which had then a population of around 1,500.

All this dynamism and "git up and go" alarmed Wade, whose efforts over the last eleven years had achieved those ten solitary piles on the foreshore. He therefore hired the old Congregational chapel for a public meeting, of which he was chairman, to expound the benefits which his Pier Company would bring to Hornsea. Unfortunately, that same night, a fire broke out at his brickyard and the meeting came hurriedly to an end. The newspaper account the next day was solely concerned with the damage to the brickyard equipment and the estimated cost of the repairs.

The legal contest between the two rivals, which had been expensively debated by their solicitors, was, in June 1877 brought before a committee of the House of Commons. The two claimant companies, the Hornsea Pier Company (North) of Wade and the Hornsea Pier, Promenade and General Improvement Company (South) of du Gillon were told by the chairman of the committee that if the two companies would agree to both piers being built then both Bills would be passed but if there was opposition from either, only one Bill would be passed. Neither contestant could have felt certain of victory since after a recess they decided not to contest the other's application and the two Bills were duly passed. The result was that Hornsea, population 1,685 at the last census, might possibly have two piers within 800 yards of one another. In contrast to the situation in Hornsea, the neighbouring resort Withernsea had opened its pier to the public that summer with great satisfaction to all concerned.

Du Gillon went ahead with his plan and signed contracts in August for the building of the sea wall defences for his South Cliff pier and harbour and the work got under way. Unfortunately the machinery and equipment on the cliffside for building the wall, as well as quantities of bricks, etc., were washed away in a storm that November, exactly as had happened to Mr. Wade in 1870. Du Gillon had come to live in Hornsea and in 1878 he was voted onto the Local Board of Health, (the chairman being Wade,) and in the August he was elected onto the committee of the Hornsea Regatta. He was still a member of the Local Board in April 1879 when his Hornsea Pier, Promenade and General Improvement Company of which he had been the chairman was declared bankrupt and was wound up. Du Gillon gave as the reason for the failure of his company the cost of litigation in the battle between the pier companies. His fellow directors testified to his probity and congratulated him on his gentlemanly conduct in the past four years. Perhaps their good opinion of him was some consolation to him as he retired from the arena defeated. In 1881 he had the occupation of ship builder in Falmouth, Cornwall. This too appears to have failed and he moved to the West Riding, where he earned his living by teaching French.

Unfortunately, Wade saw fit to write a triumphant letter to the Hornsea Gazette on this occasion. Fate, however had a surprise in store for Mr. Wade. His company had signed contracts for the building of a pier and a firm, Messrs. G. Bergheim and Co., began work in the summer of 1878; the engineer in charge, Mr. Birch, having built piers at Brighton, Margate, Scarborough and Dover.

The confidence of the public in Wade's Pier Company had not been improved by the very public contest between the two rivals; at the Annual General Meeting in March 1879, Wade complained that much less than expected had been subscribed and that promises of subscription had been broken. "The long period of apathy on the part of Hornsea people and the severe and vexatious opposition in Parliament and of the opposition from people outside Hornsea," had all been responsible for the small capital available of £8,700.

By August 1879 the original contractors were petitioning for the liquidation of the Pier Company in order to realise funds to pay their workmen and in the November the supervising engineer, Eugenius Birch, also lodged claims against the company for pay. Another firm of contractors, Messrs. De Fontaine and Co., finished constructing the pier, and in May 1880 this firm applied in the Chancery Division for a manager and a receiver to be appointed and this was done. According to the Annual General Meeting of that year the Company owed £3,500 in legal fees and had costs about £32,000, over and above the sum subscribed. Although completed, the pier remained shut during the summer of 1880.

Matters stood thus on the night of October 28th when fate dealt Mr. Wade its final blow, for this was the night of an appalling storm which raged along the north-east coast, causing dozens of ship wrecks and the damaging of both the Withernsea and Hornsea piers. For ten days before the 28th a large number of sailing ships had been lying wind-bound in the Humber. The morning of the 28th had dawned bright and sunny with a strong westerly breeze. The ships left the Humber and that afternoon 190 ships passed Withernsea with sails spread in the sunshine. No one watching that peaceful afternoon scene could have foretold that by daybreak next day 50 ships would be wrecked or run aground along Bridlington Bay.

At about 7 p.m. the wind veered suddenly to north-north-east and increased almost to hurricane force. Ships were driven helplessly towards the shore, including the brig, *Earl of Derby*, which was sailing in ballast from Le Havre, France to Seaham, County Durham.

The Hull Packet described what happened next.

"The vessel was driving before the storm on her beam ends. The captain ordered both anchors to be got ready to let go, but the gale blowing so hard the order was countermanded and it was deemed best to run in shore, so as to save life. Orders were given to look out for a red and green light, the ship being in broken water became altogether unmanageable. Shortly after Hornsea Pier was seen on the port bow and the man at the wheel put the helm hard-a-port. The vessel did not answer to her helm and the waves dashed her against the pier."

The storm seemed just as fearsome to the people of Hornsea as, with incredible gallantry, the crew of the lifeboat attempted to go to the rescue of the ships which could be seen in distress amongst the huge waves. From the Hull Packet again comes this description of the scene from the shore at Hornsea.

"Hundreds hurried from their houses to the beach. The night was pitch dark, but by the aid of a few feeble lights here and there, it could be seen that the waves were running mountains high, whilst boiling surf was being thrown up to the beach far and wide. The bell of the lifeboat house was rung and the men hurried to their duty but for some time it was impossible to get horses for the purpose of bringing the lifeboat on to the scene. Although six powerful horses were obtained and a start was effected very little progress was made, however, the animals being unable to face the wind. Torrents of rain were also falling and the sand was being blown in all directions. The result was that the attempt to get the boat to the beach was given up in despair. If it could have been taken there, it is declared there would have been insuperable difficulties in launching it on account of the huge breakers. Rockets were sent up and in one instance a line was thrown across a vessel but it did not appear to be of much use to those on board, It is stated that a vessel in the offing was burning lights as a signal of distress. These lights suddenly disappeared. It could not be ascertained what became of the ship. Later on the pier attendant went to put the light at the head of the pier but he could not walk upright. Whilst creeping along one of his hands suddenly slipped into space and he found that a large portion of the pier had been destroyed."

After the collision the mate and three seamen of the *Earl of Derby* managed to clamber onto the pier; later, the rest of the crew were rescued at 3 a.m. by the Coastguards. On inspecting the pier it was discovered that the head of the pier, 92 feet in length and 120 feet of the rest of the pier had been destroyed, leaving some 750 feet of the original 1072 feet long pier still standing.

On the following Sunday the parish magazine records that the crews of the *Earl of Derby* and the *Macbeth,* (stranded on the shore at

Atwick,) gave thanks for their escape from death at morning service at St. Nicholas church.

With the agreement of the receiver, the wrecked part of the pier was demolished and the remaining 720 feet was checked and repaired. The pier finally opened to the public on Saturday 6th August 1881, just in time for August Bank Holiday. Thereafter it opened each year between Whit Monday and the end of September. However, it never made money because the expected numbers of paying visitors never materialised and there were still outstanding debts, principally lawyers' fees. In addition, the pier was expensive to maintain and keep in good repair. Joseph Wade died in 1896 and the following year the Hornsea Pier Company was wound up and the structure was sold to a company from Manchester, to be scrapped. The last season was in 1897 and in the Autumn of that year the pier was demolished, although the entrance pavilion survived until between the World Wars.

View of the damaged Hornsea Pier after the great storm in October 1880. It was decided to open the remains of the structure to the public.

The pier opened to paying customers in August 1881. It opened every summer season until 1897, when it was scrapped.

20 Victorian Hornsea

Local Government

After the enactment of the Enclosures in 1809 and the consequent diminishing of the role of the Manor Court, a Town Meeting was formed to deal with local affairs. The Town Meetings were originally held, according to Bedell, in each of the town inns in turn, but in the staider Victorian era they were held in the vestry of the Parish Church. Members were summoned to the meetings by the tolling of the church bell. After the opening of the National School in 1845, meetings were held there, although the election of officers was still held annually in the vestry. John Wade was chairman of the Town Meeting for several years until his death in 1850.

The Town Meeting was responsible for the maintenance of the roads in the parish, and for many years the carting of stones to effect repairs was apportioned each Spring amongst the farmers of the parish. The idea of a New Road to the sea originated in 1848, and was approved by the Town Meeting, although they lacked the necessary funds to pay for the work. The road was in fact paid for by public subscription, much to the disgust of the owner of the Marine Hotel who foresaw a decrease in traffic past his hotel. Eastgate was until that time the only road down to the sea.

Also in 1848 a policeman was appointed in Hornsea with responsibility for keeping the peace at Atwick, Seaton and Sigglesthorne, but a suggestion for building a police station with cells was turned down. The Town Meeting was responsible for levying the Poor Rates, Highway and Police Rates on householders in the parish and in 1859 it had the additional task of appointing Assessors of Taxes for Property and Income Tax - a delicate situation in such a small community.

In 1863 it was suggested that a gasworks could be built and controlled by the parish, and the town lit by gas. This very modern idea received no support however, and it was left to private enterprise in the person of J. A. Wade to form the Hornsea Gas Light and Coke Co. Ltd. in 1864 with gasworks near the Hornsea Bridge station. By 1870 the number of public lights along the town streets was thirty, and the Gas Company was able to reduce the price of gas to 6 shillings per 1,000 cubic feet. This company had a rival after 1870 in the Lansdowne Gas Company in the north of the town which had gasworks near what is now Hartley Street and a gasholder on the site of what became Granville Court. It supplied the Marine Drive and Esplanade area with lighting.

The Local Government Act was adopted in Hornsea and a Local Board of Health was formed with twelve elected members and the previous Town Meeting then reverted to a Parish Council. The adoption of the Local Government Act had been opposed however by a number of residents and an appeal against the Act was heard by an Inspector in February 1864. The proceedings lasted for four hours and at the end the Inspector was moved to remark, "I have never presided at such an unruly meeting or one where so many personalities had been used." However, the appeal against adopting the Act was dismissed.

One of the first acts of the new Local Board was to improve drainage in the town. As well as undertaking the clearing out of an open drain near the National School, the Board instructed the Bellman, as the town crier was known locally, to, "... go round the town to give notice to householders that they desist from throwing offensive matter into the streets." Later that year cesspools throughout the town were cleaned out and the "night soil" carted by contractors and sold to neighbouring farmers. These primitive methods of sanitation resulted in an endemic amount of stomach infection in the town. The Hornsea Gazette each week carried advertisements by the local druggists for pills and medicines for diarrhoea, dysentery and cholera. In 1875 a deep drainage system was laid throughout the main streets of the town at a cost of £9,000.

The second problem tackled by the Local Board was the water supply. Until then, surface water in streams, shallow springs tapped by wells, or the Mere had been the only water supply available. Some of the wells had been fitted with pumps, and one of these is mentioned in an entry in the Manor Court Rolls in 1812. The first offer of a public water supply came in 1874 from J. A. Wade who had found spring water at 130 feet at his brickyard six years earlier. This offer was not taken up by the Board however, and several bore holes were drilled elsewhere. The site finally chosen for the town water supply was at Leys Hill on Atwick Road and land was bought there for a waterworks.

Coincidentally a newly formed Burial Board was considering a site for a new cemetery. The first choice for a cemetery was next door to the proposed waterworks site. Opponents of the Burial Board pointed out that standing water was reached at eight feet and the idea of a new cemetery here was abandoned after a heated controversy. By 1878 a well 265 feet deep was dug on the Leys Hill site and a pumping station, still standing today, built at a total cost of £10,000. Those who could not afford to have piped water to their homes could draw water from standpipes, or the "Town Pumps," as they were called. There was one of these pumps in Newbegin, one down Southgate, one in the Market Place and one in Golden Square, (now Bank Street.) The new water supply was first used to flush the town sewers in 1880.

The installation of these necessary services for the town was not before time. A great deal of building took place after the opening of the railway and the population nearly doubled between 1861 and 1871. Many of the houses forming the Grosvenor Estate near the station, Railway Street, New Road, Park Road and Eastbourne Road were built between 1870 and 1880, as were some of the houses in the Lansdowne Estate, which included Cliff Lane, (now Cliff Road,) and the Esplanade. Suffolk Terrace, on Seaton Road, also dates from this period, as does Gothic Terrace in Westgate.

The first Marine Hotel was pulled down in 1874 because of the erosion of the cliffs and the present, somewhat smaller building erected. In 1875 the Coastguard Station in front of Marine Drive became uninhabitable also because of erosion, and cottages for the coastguardsmen were built in Cliff Lane, now 6 to 11 Cliff Road. (These cottages were inspected on August 16th 1881 by H.R.H. the Duke of Edinburgh, a younger son of Queen Victoria, who landed from the yacht *Lively*, whilst the town's brass band played, and then drove in J. A. Wade's carriage to the cottages and inspected the Coastguards.)

This was followed in 1879 by the sale of the old lifeboat house built in 1864, which used to be on the shore between New Road and Sands Lane, and the building of a much larger one at the corner of Eastbourne Road and Burton Road. In 1900 a Hornsea Volunteer Rocket Life Saving Brigade was formed to help the lifeboatmen in their rescue work.

The first office of the Hornsea Local Board of Health was in Chambers Lane, although the monthly meetings of the board were held in the National School. By 1881 however a boardroom and office was established in the Public Rooms in Newbegin, (later the Star Cinema, and in in 2002, Hornsea Library.) As well as a clerk, the Board had by then a medical officer and a surveyor.

Although the town now had water and drainage and the streets were lit by gas lamps, the roads were still surfaced with stone chippings, or "metal" as it was called. The pavements around the Market Place had cobble paving, but elsewhere they were gravelled. This road surface was churned up into mud in winter and dried out to dust in summer. When John Heslop, a druggist with a shop in the Market Place, put stone flags on the path in front of his premises in 1877 he was commended for his public spirit. The rest of the town pavements remained cobbled until November 1901. The year 1877 also saw the planting of two fine trees in the Bull Ring and in June the first electric lighting was introduced into the town.

In 1884 it was decided, after 20 years of argument, that a new burial ground must be found. Two acres of land and the old farm buildings, still called the White House, in Southgate, were bought for £1,000. It was decided that a mortuary chapel should be built to the right of the entrance to the cemetery and a board room on the left of the entrance. This curious arrangement was completed by June 1885 at a cost of £300. That year too the Waterworks were extended and improved, and finally a police station was provided for Hornsea in the Market Place.

With all these modern developments there still remained remnants of the pastoral age. The Harvest Bell was rung in the evening in September until 1881 and as late as 1895 tenders for the "letting of the sweep of the scythes" for certain of the roads was advertised. The Manorial Court Leet lingered on, still appointing the Steward of the Manor, the Lord's Steward and the Bailiff of the Court, although their only duty seemed to be to attend a Court Leet dinner held annually at one of the hotels. This custom gradually faded out about 1910.

Social Life

The coming of the railway in 1864 made it possible for commuters to live in Hornsea and many well-to-do families moved out from Hull. This led to a great increase in the social life of the town. The publishing of the Hornsea Gazette from 1869 meant that all the events of Interest in the small town were recorded in detail, giving a fascinating record of the vitality of that era. For the sports loving section of the community several new activities were provided. A Cricket Club formed in 1867 played on land owned by Mr. J.A. Wade alongside the railway station. Mr. Wade was President of the Club and organised Cricket Weeks in the summer when visiting batsmen were entertained at Hornsea House, Eastgate. It was during one of these Cricket Weeks that the famous Dr. W.G. Grace played at Hornsea in a match in June 1874. A team of twenty-two Hornsea players, including their professional Briggs, played against a United South of England XI. In the first innings the eminent doctor was caught by the bowler for 11. His team made 44 against the Hornsea team's 86. Fortunately for the Doctor's temper he scored 58 out of a total of 161 in the second innings when the Hornsea score was 86 again. Interest in cricket was so keen that in the next season another club was started - the Hornsea and East Holderness Cricket Club, which played on land in Southorpe Road. The two clubs remained separate until 1900 when a United Cricket Club was formed. For the ladies a Tennis Club was formed in 1879 which played on part of the cricket ground and there was also a Cycling Club in the eighties and by 1899 on Association Football Club too.

For the martially inclined a company of the East Yorkshire Artillery Volunteers was raised in December 1864. These Volunteers drilled in a drill room at the Old Hotel, (Low Hall in 2002,) on three nights in the week and in 1869 a brass band was formed. The Artillery Volunteers' annual ball held in the Public Rooms was one of the highlights of the Hornsea year. In 1884 a drill hall in Back Southgate was built for the Volunteers, which was enlarged in 1890 to give as well as the hall, a parade ground, a band room and an armoury. The armoury included two 32 pound cannons on garrison carriages. These were used for shooting practice on the sands north of the Marine Hotel and remained some years after the disbanding of the Volunteers, one on the Bull Ring and one on the Promenade North Cliff.

Musical interest in Hornsea was provided by concerts given during the season by the Town Brass Band. From 1870 onwards musical promenades were held during the season in the grounds of the newly built Alexandra Hotel and also on the North Cliff. A Vocal Society was formed in 1874 and a Choral Association in 1882. Both of these societies gave concerts in the Public Rooms.

The gardeners of the town had the Hornsea Floral and Horticultural Society Show, President Mr. J.A. Wade, which was held in a field next to Hornsea House. This was held each June from 1870 to 1914.

Perhaps the prime event of the year though was the Hornsea Regatta and Aquatic Sports, held every August Bank Holiday Monday from 1876 until the First World War. The programme consisted of yacht races and rowing boat races as well as an "Aquatic Horse Race" in which competitors sat in a wooden tub with a wooden horse's head fixed on the front and paddled to victory. On the shore obstacle races, 3-legged races, tug-of-war and egg and spoon races were held. These Aquatic Sports attracted very large crowds to the town and the excursion trains were kept running until 2 a.m. the next day. The popularity of the event is evident from this newspaper account of 1881:-

"The sands were crowded with holiday makers, flags flying, bands playing and singing parties abroad from noon till late at night. These were supplied by the Salvation Army who paraded the streets of the town and marched up and down on the sands with banners flying and the Primitive Methodists who assembled in great force from Hull and District. In the evening a grand display of fireworks by Dr. Browne, (pyrotechnist to the Hull Botanic Gardens,) took place in a field behind the Old Hotel, Southgate."

The Public Rooms in Newbegin, built in 1869, provided the setting for a great deal of indoor entertainment in the 'eighties and 'nineties. In 1882 came a visit from Miss Constance St. Clare and her theatrical company who provided a programme of plays such as "Lady Audley's Secret," "East Lynne" and "Dick Turpin" - concluding the evening programme with a "laughable farce." A great many balls and dances took place there, as well as the usual fundraising concerts for various local organizations. These were varied in the 'nineties by "Negro Minstrel" entertainments which were very popular. Some long standing events in the Hornsea calendar were disappearing however. The traditional horse races were still being held on the sands north of the Marine Hotel annually until 1885, although they seemed to need the addition of bicycle races and donkey races to make up a programme. The weekly market, which had been held for over 600 years petered out after the opening of the railway, as had the winter cattle fair by 1877.

Local Employment

The Autumn Statute Hirings were still held on the first Monday after Martinmas when the farmers would hire their men and women labourers for the coming year. The men would stand around the Market Place waiting to be hired. So did the women until the building of the Parish Room in 1887 when they were allowed to wait there. Stalls selling sweets and gingerbread were set out in the Market Place and the public houses had their busiest time of the year. Wages for lads were £5 - £6 a year. Men earned £15 to £18 and women £12 to £18. After agreeing to hire a man the farmer would give him 1 shilling as "fest" money which sealed the bargain.

Many of the remaining cottagers still kept a pig and had vegetable gardens too. The killing of the pig was one of the high spots of the year. This traditionally took place on 17th December. After the slaughter of the pig at the butcher's, the carcass was cut up and small joints and portions of "pig's fry" were sent to friends and relations. Nothing was wasted; the blood would be made into black pudding and other delicacies such as brawn and sausages were made too.

Nearly all of the winters of the last quarter of the 19th century were extremely cold. On two occasions between 1875 and 1884 the ice froze to such a depth that an ox was roasted on the Mere. Mr. Heslop who farmed at Southorpe Farm was able to drive his pony cart across the Mere to the Market Place and bricks from Wade's brickyard were pulled across the ice on a sledge for the building of 27 Westgate, (Grebe House.) When the ice froze in 1890 a cricket match was played on the ice on Boxing Day and a sheep roasted as well. These hard winters were times of near starvation and hardship for the poor. The Parish Magazine records the attempts by the wealthier members of the community to relieve this suffering and in one month in 1879, 80 quarts of soup with bread were distributed. A coal club was also formed to buy coal for the poor and that same year 43 tons of coal were given away. As soon as the frosts were over, the half starved labourers had to return to work for the food distribution stopped.

One of the main employers of the town's labour force was the Hornsea Brick and Tile Works owned by Mr. J.A. Wade which was established in 1864. The brickyard, with its five-sailed windmill, (an unusual feature instead of the more usual four,) that supplied the power, and the cottages and the kiln with its tall chimney stack were landmarks in Hornsea. The windmill had two round millstones which were used end-on to grind the clay into a fine state. The tubs of clay were brought upon tracks from the clay pit to the mill. The worked clay was transferred to sheds nearby for moulding and baking. One of these mill wheels is still lying in Hall Garth Park. A "Patent Interlocking

Roofing Tile" was made there, examples of which can be seen on the walls of Grosvenor House, New Road. This successful brickyard had a rival enterprise in the north of the town. In 1873 a brickyard called the Hornsea Steam Brick and Tile Works was begun on 9 acres of land north of Seaton Road, (at the Seaton end of Suffolk Terrace.) These brickworks possessed a pugmill and presses for the bricks and could produce 3,000 bricks at a time. The management of this brickyard was viewed with disfavour by local employers since wages were offered there of £30 to £40 a year, or double the agricultural wage. Perhaps it was this factor which led to the bankruptcy of the brickworks in 1881 and the removal of another of the business rivals of Mr. Wade.

After playing a leading role in the life of the town for 40 years, Joseph Armytage Wade died in 1896 at the age of 78. Eastgate House was bought by the wealthy trawler owner, Christopher Pickering, who took over many of the public offices previously held by Mr. Wade. Mr. Pickering built the Almshouses, Newbegin, on the site of the old parish cottages.

A few men were able to earn a living by fishing and crabbing. After the opening of the railway the increased demand for fish and shell fish for the visitors to the town and the opportunity to earn money from sailing trips, etc., during the season led to a few cobles fishing from Hornsea. The fishermen were also able to supplement their incomes by having small booths on the sands for the sale of cooked shrimps, crabs, etc., as well as tea for holiday makers. According to a directory, there were 12 fishermen sailing from Hornsea in 1892.

Friendly Societies

At a time when there was little or no health insurance available, the friendly societies had an important role to play. The first of these mutual aid societies in Hornsea, according to Bedell, was the Oddfellows. A second friendly society, the Victoria Lodge of the Ancient Order of Druids, (Hull District,) was formed in the winter of 1862 with the Reverend Wood of Atwick as chairman, and Mr. Denton as surgeon to the Lodge. There were some 60 members of the Lodge and a small weekly payment gave some insurance cover against loss of earnings due to sickness. By 1892 the "Druids," as they were commonly called, had 233 members and met monthly at the Victoria. The lodge was known as the "Perseverance Lodge." For many years the Druids would be at the head of the town parades, members wearing their full regalia and chains of office as can be see from many old photographs. Another friendly society, The United Order of British Workmen, formed a branch in Hornsea in 1873. This society also held meetings at the Victoria but had only 27 members in the "Fruitful Vine Lodge." Both societies were active at the end of the 19th century.

The Freemasons were first introduced into Hornsea in association with the Alexandra Hotel. This was opened in 1869 and an Alexandra

Lodge of Freemasons was formed by 1875. The Masonic meetings were held at the Hotel until 1899, when the Alexandra Lodge, built in Alexandra Road at a cost of £650, was opened by the Marquess of Zetland.

Final Changes in Local Government

The monthly meetings of the Local Board, formed in 1864, were held after 1885 in the newly built board room at the entrance to the Southgate Cemetery. Meetings for the full board were on the first Monday of the month. The twelve members were divided into three main committees, a Burial & Sanitary Committee, and a Waterworks Committee, both of which met on the Thursday before the board meetings and a Highways Committee which met on the Friday previous to board meetings. There was also a Lighting Committee but this met only occasionally. There were two officers to the board - a Clerk and a Surveyor and voting for the election of members to the Board was held in the Public Rooms, Newbegin. A list of public officials for Hornsea given in the 1892 East Riding Directory shows a fascinating mixture of the old world and the new- Assessor and Collector of Income Tax, Steward of the Manor Court, Medical Officer and Public Vaccinator, Churchwarden, Collector of Poor Rates, Feoffees of the Church Lands, Registrar of Births, Marriages & Deaths, Parish Clerk, Poor Law Guardian, and the Town Crier. The last named official was also the Town Pinder and had the duty of collecting animals straying on the highway and keeping them in the pinfold. After the enclosures, the pinfold was on Fair Place alongside the National School. The last Town Crier always wore a billycock, (a type of bowler,) hat when crying the notices through the town and he would add the words, "Noo dean't forgit it!" to the end of every announcement. The Local Board was superseded in 1895 by the formation of the Hornsea Urban District Council.

The Diamond Jubilee, 1897

The 60th anniversary of the accession of Queen Victoria was of course a great day to celebrate. In Hornsea the day began with a triumphant peal of the church bells at 8 a.m. followed at 8.30 a.m. by the singing of two hymns and the National Anthem by a group of choristers from the top of the Church tower.

At 12 noon the Hornsea Artillery Volunteers fired a salvo on Fair Place and at 2 p.m. a long procession led by the Artillery band started from Mereside. After the band came the Coastguards carrying the standard followed by the Artillery Volunteers, and Hornsea Urban District Council members. Next came the town brass band, the two friendly societies with junior "Druids" dressed in druids' robes riding on horses, and finally some 40 decorated cycles. After parading through the town the procession turned into Hall Garth Park. Here all the children of the town were presented with a Jubilee mug and medal by Mr. and Mrs. A. Maw (Mr. Maw was a director of the Hull drapers, Maw, Till and Kirk and lived at Grosvenor House, New Road.) The presentations were followed by tea for the 450 children in the Public Rooms; for the elderly tea was provided in the Congregational and Wesleyan schoolrooms. At 6 p.m. sports began on Kirkholme Point and these were followed by a bonfire and fireworks display at 10 p.m.

As a more permanent memorial of the Jubilee two improvement schemes were undertaken. The first scheme was to widen the road at the junction of Market Place and Newbegin. The so-called market cross which had stood in the middle of the road had been moved to Mr. Heslop's farm at Southorpe some years before and left in the farmyard there. Four cottages which stood in the corner of the churchyard were pulled down and the road widened. The cross was re-erected in the churchyard on the site of the cottages. The cost of all these improvements was shared by the church, (£250,) a public subscription, (£200,)and the Hornsea Urban District Council, (£100.) The   second scheme was the buying and laying out of the Jubilee Gardens on the North Cliff. The land was purchased by a group of local gentlemen for £2,000 and a public subscription raised £150 to lay out the land as a public garden. On either side of the broad walk leading from the main entrance was a tennis court or bowling green and a narrow border of flowers edged the walk itself. (Later in 1913 the Floral Hall was built in the gardens.) In July 1898 there was a formal opening of the Jubilee Garden and the unveiling of the Market Place cross on the same day before crowds of spectators.

The Seaside

The opening of the railway made a great deal of difference to the type of visitor coming to Hornsea. A day return ticket cost 1 shilling in those days and with the facility of cheap travel it became possible for all but the very poor to go for the day to the seaside. Obviously the catering provided for these visitors would differ from that of the Marine Hotel and other similar establishments. The "Refreshment Saloon" on the sands could offer prices that most could afford:-

First Class Tea with Ham	1 shilling
Plain Tea	8d
Children's Tea	6d
Cup of Tea	1d
Cup of Coffee	1d

The number of lodging and boarding houses multiplied after the opening of the railway until there were some 100 lodging houses available to visitors by the end of the century. Most of the lodging houses were at first in Newbegin, Southgate and the Mereside, but later with the development of Cliff Road, the Esplanade and Marine Drive these areas became more popular. Prices for accommodation ranged from £1 to 10s a week for "Apartments," i.e., rooms with service, to 5s 6d a day at the Alexandra Hotel. The development of a specially designed bathing dress in the 1890's meant that visitors could indulge in mixed bathing with propriety. This had not always been the case. The original sea bathers had been towed out to sea in horse drawn bathing machines to a short distance from the shore. The men bathers would customarily not wear a costume, at least according to one complaint from a Scarborough newspaper in 1863, "... men are allowed to bathe in a state of nudity with machines at the waters edge with water only up to their knees." Complaint was made that under the circumstances the ladies' and gentlemen's machines were too close together for propriety. A similar situation at Hornsea led to a bye-law proposed by Mr. Wade in November 1864, "That the male and female bathers be separated, the one machine to be not less than 200 yards from the other."

Hornsea never developed as a seaside resort on a large scale. Withernsea and Bridlington were both quicker to exploit their potential. Both had railway lines years before Hornsea. and both benefited from the economic power of day trippers.

The people of Hornsea seemed quite content with their town and the many interests and societies that were available. Attractions for visitors were limited to the natural pleasures of the beach with a few brass band concerts and pierrot shows. From 1885 the Mere was opened for boating and fishing but the natural beauty of the Mere was never commercialised. Although one of the first acts of the newly formed Hornsea Urban District Council in 1895 was to form a Promenade Improvement Committee, the subsequent Jubilee Gardens were 40 years later than the ornamental gardens at Withernsea. Looking through the newspaper accounts of the last quarter of the 19th century it seems that Hornsea had settled down to a placid routine with a summer season of events like the Regatta, garden parties and Sunday School treats, followed by the winter concerts and dances.

One of the few interruptions to this calm progress through the years was the outbreak of the Boer War in October 1899, when six men from the Hornsea Company of Artillery Volunteers volunteered for service in South Africa. But Africa was very far away and perhaps the idea put forward for the building of a tramway to run through the town from the railway station to Atwick Road caused more excitement that winter. Queen Victoria's death in 1901 seemed to bring no change in the continuity of town life. The return of three of the volunteers at the end of the Boer War in 1902 was celebrated by a parade from barracks to a thanksgiving service in the church. The coronation of King Edward VII that August was celebrated by the usual town parade, children's tea and the gift of Coronation mugs and medals. Many of the larger houses were decorated with electric lights and "transparencies," and the Promenade

Gardens had illuminations. An Austrian Blue Band played a popular selection of Viennese waltzes, and Naval rockets from the Coastguard Station were let off too. As the onlookers made their way home from the celebrations it must have seemed that nothing could change; the future, they felt, could hold only peace and prosperity.

The Population of Hornsea in the 19th Century

1801	533
1811	704
1821	790
1831	780
1841	1005
1851	945
1861	1063
1871	1685
1881	1836
1891	2013

The Jubilee Gardens were opened in 1898 to mark Queen Victoria's Diamond Jubilee the previous year. This picture is taken from a postcard which shows the scene after a storm in March 1906. It was this erosion which prompted the building of Hornsea's first sea wall.

Some Buildings of Interest

THE CHURCH OF ST. NICHOLAS   (Picture on page 14)

The church of St. Nicholas, built mainly in the last quarter of the 14th century, stands on a hill which even today dominates the town centre. A church is mentioned in Domesday Book, 1086. That first Saxon church might possibly have been built upon the site of a pagan building, for pagans too chose high places for their temples.

The building, completed by the Abbey of St. Mary's York, has known several vicissitudes. There are references in papers belonging to the Borthwick Institute, York, to repairs necessary in 1461 to the south wall of the church. The wooden spire which surmounted the tower was, according to a memorandum in the church register, blown down in 1714 and the church roof was blown off in the hurricane of December 23rd 1732. Bedell says that the south aisle was re-roofed in about 1827, the north aisle and chancel re-roofed in 1845, and also that the room at the west end of the south aisle was used as a schoolroom.

The Victorian architect Sir Gilbert Scott supervised an extensive restoration of the church in 1868 when the battlements of the tower were raised and the eight stone pinnacles were added in place of the four weather vanes which had previously been on each corner. It was at the time of this restoration that a seal with the inscription "Sigillum de S. Catherine" was said to have been dug up near the south side of the church.

The Vicarage

An ancient vicarage stood in front of the present vicarage. The old building is believed to have been destroyed by fire about 1785. Its replacement was demolished at the beginning of the incumbency of Anthony Eyre, who was vicar from 1831 to 1849, and the present vicarage was built. The Reverend Eyre's son, Edward John Eyre, sailed for Australia at the age of 18 and spent several years as an overlander driving cattle from the interior to the coast. In 1840 he set out with four companions from Adelaide and during a year of incredible hardship walked across the continent to Albany. On the way he discovered a hitherto unknown lake which was named Lake Eyre in his honour. He published an account of his travels, "Discoveries in Central Australia," which made him a celebrity. He became a colonial governor and died on November 30th 1901.

The Parish Room
This was built in 1887 to mark Queen Victoria's Golden Jubilee. The cost of the building, some £200, was raised by the Parish.

QUAKER COTTAGE, BACK WESTGATE

(Picture on page 52)

One of the buildings still in existence with an early recorded history seems to be the building now known as Quaker Cottage in Back Westgate. The first mention of this cottage in the Manor Court Rolls is in 1640 when Robert Moore, "... died seized of 5½ oxgangs of land, 2 cottages in Southgate, half a boon in Westgate and a parcel of a cottage in Westgate called a Garnew and a cottage called Westclose." The Moore family leased the Manor of Hornsea from the Crown for some years from 1597, probably until the Commonwealth, 1649-1660. The parcel of a cottage called a "Garnew" was in fact a large barn, (or a garner,) and it is interesting that this is the only barn referred to as a garner in the Manor Court Rolls. The cottage was situated at the end of the lane which separated the East and West Fields, known in the 17th century as Bitchis Lane and it had a narrow rectangular enclosure, (or close,) which encompassed the area between Back Westgate and Westgate. When the owner of the Rectory was also the impropriator of the Rectorial Tithes those could have been stored in a barn near the Rectory. It is a possibility that the "Garnew" could have served to store the Rectorial Tithes on occasions when the Rectory house was not owned by the impropriator of the tithes.

The property in Westgate was taken over by Thomas Acklam in 1653 and the barn was subsequently used as a Quaker meeting house according to an entry in the Manor Court Rolls of 1750 describing, "... a barn or garth adjoining upon Bitchis Lane being one cottage and a Garnor or Meeting House." In 1785 in the will of Peter Acklam are details showing that the barn was still used as a meeting place but the cottage was by now used as a stable and there was also, "... the yard now used as a Burying ground for the said people called Quakers." The only identifiable property which might have been earlier than Quaker Cottage was the White House.

THE WHITE HOUSE, SOUTHGATE (Demolished)

The first mention of the White House in the Manor Court Rolls is in 1629 when Edward Chawlis surrendered the property to Robert Moore. (The Moore family leased the Manor of Hornsea for many years.) The property passed to a glover, Francis Coulson, in 1654 and it remained in the Coulson family until 1704 when it was surrendered to Peter Acklam. It is worth noting that this property had an entirely separate, well-documented existence because of a confusion which arose towards the end of the 19th century when the name "The White House" came to be mistakenly applied to Low Hall, Southgate. The real White House in 1722 was tenanted by John Barnes who owned other property nearby which was described in the Manor Court Rolls as, "... a cottage in Southgate near Gildas Hill commonly called White House and two cottages joining on ffootball greene." The reason why the property came to be called the White House may lie in its use. A tannery had been developed on the north bank of Stream Dyke in Southgate; tanning requires large quantities of quicklime and it may be that the drifts of white powder on the paths and around the lime pits gave rise to the name.

In 1719 Francis Coulson surrendered half of his house called White House in Southgate, "... with 7½ yards of the Garth from the N.W. corner of the orchard wall fronting the street to the South west corner of ye said White House." This entry indicates that the property was on the north side of Southgate. Further details occur in an entry of 1734 when Mary Foster, "... surrenders the White House with yard and outhouses belonging to the beck thereof," showing that the cottage stood on the side of the beck, (now called Stream Dyke). The tannery seems to have discontinued, for by 1747, "... the White house with a Kilne," (used for brewing,) is surrendered. In 1756 John Brough of Rolston gentleman, acquires, "... a cottage near Gildass Hill called White House," and the last entry in the Manor Court Rolls is in 1779 when John Bedell takes over the White House.

The property was still in existence in January 1884 as witness a paragraph in the Hornsea Gazette which refers to a stack fire in Robert Heron's farm yard opposite the White House. It was feared that the flames would spread to a row of six cottages alongside the farm yard however John Heslop, living nearby, put the flames out. The White House together with two acres of land alongside the farm buildings were bought in March 1884 by the Local Board of Health for £1,000. In July that year it was decided to pull down the buildings and build the cemetery chapel and boardroom for the Local Board of Health on the site.

LOW HALL, SOUTHGATE   (Picture on page 52)

In January 1665 John Newsom and Elinor his wife surrendered a cottage, "... called a Low Close" in Southgate to Thomas Acklam with access with cart and carriage." Two years later, on the death of Thomas Acklam, it is listed among his property and described still as a cottage. Bedell says that the Low Hall was built in 1674 and that a knocker with that date used to be on the door. However in the Manor Court Rolls in May 1675 Peter Acklam surrenders, "... one cottage to George Pattison." In November of that year comes the entry, "Peter Acklam the elder surrenders three cottages in Southgate wherein George Pattison now dwelleth provided that the new garden plot and part of the three cottages in Southgate with free ingress and egress and regress into the same be returned to the use of the said Peter Acklam and Alice his wife, Peter Acklam and Thomas Acklam his sons and Anna Maria his daughter for a burying plot when and as often as they or any of them shall desire the same." From this entry it seems that the cottage Low Close was enlarged and a garden marked out in the summer of 1675. When Peter Acklam died in 1691 and his wife later in 1692 they were buried in the garden of this house. The Pattison family were tenants of one of the cottages till 1709. The other three cottages seemed to have formed Low Hall or so it would seem from an entry in 1730 made shortly before the death of Anna Maria Acklam daughter of the first Peter Acklam, when she left to her nephew Peter four cottages in Hornsea, "... being the house where she now dwelleth and one other cottage in Southgate." Low Hall remained the property of the Acklam family until 1777 when Peter Acklam IV surrendered, "... a Capital Messuage or Mansion House with Stables, outbuildings, orchards, etc., situate in a place called Southgate."

Low Hall became an inn and for many years after 1806 it was known as, "The Old Hotel" to distinguish it from the New Hotel in the Market Place. The Methodists in the 1770's for a time used one of the rooms at the Old Hotel for their meetings. Around 1820 John Heslop took over the inn and he was followed as landlord by his son, also called John. During their ownership the name of the inn was sometimes varied to Heslop's Hotel and from 1846 a coach service to Hull started from the Old Hotel at 8 p.m. during the summer season. It is also during the Heslop's tenancy that an inquest was held there on the death by poisoning of a farmer and his servant at Hornsea Burton in 1837.

From 1857 Thomas Legatt was the licensee and it was in his time that the railway navvies caused so much trouble with their drunken behaviour and Mr. Leggatt had often to appear in court cases to give evidence of having beer tankards thrown at him. After the railway was opened public concerts were sometimes given in a room there to entertain visitors until the opening of the Public Rooms in 1869.

The temperance movement seems to have gained a convert in the next owner, a Mr. Coulman who, in 1875, turned the inn into a temperance hotel. He advertised in the Hornsea Gazette that his hotel, (late Old Hotel,) "... is close to the Mere and visitors to the Hotel are allowed to roam freely by its margin. For the convenience of Schools and Large Parties a spacious Saloon is provided and also an excellent cricket ground." A Mr. Witty took over the Temperance Hotel in 1880 and seems to have kept it until about 1885, as well as providing a livery stable and bait sales.

It was at this time after the demolition of the real White House that the switch of name occurred when the new owner, Mr. J. Harker, opened the White House Livery Stables and apartments. The property is now used as a private residence, which still has some Acklam family gravestones in the garden.

THE OLD HALL, MARKET PLACE

In 1651 Peter Acklam bought the Old Rectory house or Parsonage together with the "Hall Garth" from Robert Moore and it is possible that both he and his father, Thomas, lived here for several years until, in 1665, Thomas Acklam bought Low Close in Southgate. The Old Rectory was said by Bedell to have survived until the reign of James II, i.e., 1685 to 1688, when it was pulled down by Peter Acklam II.

It is difficult to fix a date for the building of the Old Hall in the Market Place. However, it is known that it was built by the Acklams. Bedell says that the house is Jacobean, i.e., built before 1625, but this must be incorrect, as is Poulson's statement that "High Hall," (to distinguish it from Low Hall,) was built by the Acklams in 1787. The Acklams lived in Hornsea from 1651 to 1760 when Peter Acklam III died without issue and his property passed to his nephew Peter Acklam of the Dringhoe branch of the family. From the style of architecture, the Dutch gables, etc., it must have been built after the Restoration in 1660 when domestic architecture was influenced by the return of the exiled Royalists from Holland. The "Information" laid by the Vicar of Hornsea in 1665 speaks of 100 people attending a meeting in Peter Acklam's house; again, the Hearth Tax returns of 1672 show him as owning a house with six hearths. Both facts are evidence of a large house but do not indicate if this was the Old Rectory or "High Hall." Some other facts may help to form an assumption about the date.

The Quakers were fined very heavily for their absence from church services and in 1678 Peter Acklam was fined £20 a month, a very large sum indeed. After the Act of Toleration in 1682 these fines ceased and in 1684 Peter Acklam was able to afford to lease the Manor of Hornsea. It seems most likely that it was after 1684 that the Hall was built. It may be that Poulson's date was a misprint and that it should have read 1687. The pulling down of the old Rectory might also be for the reason that a new brick-built Hall was ready for occupancy and that the old cobble-built Rectory was no longer

Old Hall   Hornsea

needed. From the Manor Court Rolls it seems there were three bricklayers living in Hornsea in 1700 and it may be that the bricks used for the building were made in the Westgate brickyard. However, the Hall can claim to be one of the earliest brick buildings in Hornsea and from 1687 to 1760 it was the house of the Lord of the Manor.

THE TOWER, NEWBEGIN

This 19th century folly was built in the garden of the house identified in the chapter on the Hornsea guilds as the Newbegin Guild House. The original cottage was extended to make three cottages in 1805. In 1811 a Hull merchant, George Alder, bought the property and gave the building a Georgian facade. This house was bought in 1842 by Mr. William Bettison, a brewer and part proprietor of the Hull Advertiser. In 1844 he had the tower built, so the story goes, in order that his son could climb to the top of the tower with a telescope and watch for his father's barouche coming down Southorpe Hill. The son would then ring a bell to warn the cook to have the dinner ready for serving as soon as his father walked into the dining room. Mr. Bettison was a very unpleasant man and much disliked by the townspeople. Next door to him, (at 38 Newbegin,) lived the Congregational Minister whose sailor son, home on leave, climbed up the outside of the tower one night and hung a placard saying "Bettisons Folly" on the top of the tower and as such it was known for many years after Mr. Bettison had left Hornsea. It seems that the builder of the tower visited the next owner of the property at one time and told him that the tower had cost £300 to build and that Mr. Bettison had gone bankrupt before the builder had been paid so that he never received a penny for it.

THE ASSEMBLY ROOMS, NEWBEGIN

The Assembly Room and Public Rooms were built in 1869 by the Hornsea Public Rooms Company, Ltd. The Assembly Room or Music Room was 62 feet x 36 feet and there were also four committee rooms at the front. Nearly all the public concerts, dances and public meetings in Hornsea were held there until the building of the Floral Hall in 1913. The proprietors had calculated on an increasing demand for public entertainment in Hornsea after the opening of the railways in 1864 but the resort did not expand as quickly as anticipated. Although the Artillery Volunteers held their annual ball here and the Vocal Society gave their concerts there too, the building was not a financial success. Even the opening of a Lending Library in one of the four rooms in 1872 did not solve the problem. The original owners sold the premises to a second company in 1879 but unfortunately this also became bankrupt in 1884. Through the years all the musical events in Hornsea were held

in the Assembly Room. Sacred music from the Vocal Society, President Mr. T.B. Holmes, alternated with fund raising concerts from the Hornsea Choral Association, (formed in 1882,) for such worthy events as the Hornsea Regatta. At the turn of the century came the Rainbow Choir and a children's choir to give cantatas and operettas under an enthusiastic schoolmaster-conductor, Mr. Herbert Sykes.

In the 1890's the Primitive Methodist August Bank Holiday rally would finish the day, at 1 shilling a head, in the Assembly Room, when often as many as 900 would crowd into a final prayer meeting. As well as a Lending Library in the four rooms at the front, there was at one time a Penny Bank, and a Miss Emily Hall held a private dame school there too.

After the formation of the Hornsea Urban District Council in 1895 the Council Offices occupied the top floor overlooking Newbegin. There were then only two full time officers - a Clerk and a Surveyor. The Council offices remained there until 1921 when Elim Lodge was bought for £4,000. The basement provided living accommodation for the caretaker, and at one time this post was held by a Moses Spittle.

In 1900 the first silent film show in Hornsea was given in the Assembly Room. Apparently the first film showed an express train, which to the startled audience seemed to be coming off the screen and into the hall. As was usual at that time, a pianist played an appropriate accompaniment. The building, by then known as the Star Cinema, was pulled down in 1973 and Hornsea Library now stands on the site.

THE OLD CHAPEL, SOUTHGATE

This building, which was erected in 1808, was originally the first purpose-built nonconformist chapel to be built in Hornsea and it served as the Independent chapel, (later known as the Congregational chapel.) It was known as the Bethesda Chapel. It became surplus to requirements in June 1874, when the new Congregational church building was opened in New Road. The old chapel was then taken over by the Independent Order of the Good Templars, (a temperance organisation,) from Hull and converted into a lodge room and lecture hall which opened on November 25th 1874. Several temperance meetings were held every year and the lodge was known as the Good

Templars Hope of Hornsea Lodge.

The women servants waiting to be hired at the Martinmas Hirings in November were offered accommodation there as an alternative to the Victoria Hotel. The temperance movement gained new supporters from the newly formed Church of England Temperance Society which in 1876 held a magic lantern exhibition in the Temperance Hotel, (formerly the Old Hotel,) nearby. In 1881 a "Major Thomson" of the Salvation Soldiers, (who were unconnected with the Salvation Army,) began to hold meetings in the Good Templars' Hall. The response was so great that at one Saturday meeting tea was served at 5.30 to 400 people and this was followed by an all night prayer meeting until 4.30 a.m. on Sunday. Alas, "Major Thomson" proved to be a fraud and absconded with the group's funds. Meanwhile the Templars were still providing tea and entertainment at the "Hope of Hornsea" Lodge several times a year until 1888. For some years afterwards the hall was used for dances and concerts until in 1911 it was taken over as the parish hall by St. Nicholas' Church.

After the arrival of the railway in 1864, all three nonconformist groups built new, larger chapels

PRIMITIVE METHODIST
Designed by Joseph Wright
Opened in 1864

WESLEYAN METHODIST
Designed by J.K. James
Opened in 1870

CONGREGATIONALIST
Designed by Samuel Musgrave
Opened in 1874

Appendix 2

Personal Memories

AN ACCOUNT OF HORNSEA
by
Arthur Loten
Born 1848 Written in 1928
Note: Locations in 2002, where known, are indicated in square brackets

Hornsea as I remember it and I can go back about eighty years was just a rural village with a population of about 800. I love to think of Hornsea as it was with its simple rural life, its peaceful atmosphere, its simple pleasures and amusements, its green fields and lovely gardens. It comprised Southgate, Back Southgate, the Mere-side, Market Place, Newbegin, Westgate, Back Westgate and Eastgate; that is all.

Now let us have a look first of all at **Southgate**. It was considered to be quite stylish. The shop rounding the corner of Market Place was a chemist's shop where two of my brothers served their apprenticeships. There were four chemists in our family. On the right hand side of Southgate there was a public house bearing the name of Hole in the Wall. The shop looking down Chambers Lane [6 Southgate] was a chemist's shop. Three ministers lived in Southgate. The senior Wesleyan minister lived where Walker's butchers shop is. The junior minister lived on the opposite side and the Congregational minister lived where Mr. Tabor's [Evans Jewellers] shop is. The Mission Hall was the Congregational Chapel. Mr. Gayden's house was considered to be palatial. The big old house opposite was a farmhouse. Harker's White House was the Old Hotel [Low Hall] carried on by John Heslop, the late Mr. George Heslop's father. There were three more houses on the left hand side, seven cottages on the opposite side and you were out in the country. There was a farm and gate shutting off Southgate from Rolston Road.

The **Market Place** has been transformed. There were old houses where the Argenta [Prospect Nursery] and Wheldale [Hornsea Window Brokers/S.M. Wood Building Services] shops are. There were three or four thatched cottages where the Army and Navy Stores [Train's

127

Hair and Beauty] and Mr. Fisher's [Jiffy Bar] and Mr. Hebden's [Kebab Express] are. One of them was the police station which had one policeman, a big burly fellow, a terror to children. On the opposite side of the Market Place were four tiny low cottages in the churchyard coming up to the church gate and in one was a barber's shop carried on by Benjamin West. There were two half doors into the shop; the top half was thrown back to let the light in. There were two old houses next to these cottages. Wrigglesworth's [No. 10, empty] was a druggist's and grocer's shop and was also the post office. An old house where Mr. Smith's ironmonger's shop [Eastgate Travel] is and a smithy close on the street. The New Inn, the Rose and Crown, Salmond's blacksmith shop [Shackles',] the Victoria Hotel and that was all. There was a garden where the Primitive Methodist Chapel stands and the two houses and Mr. Smith's butcher's shop [Feng Shui.] The garden ran to Atwick Road fenced in by a quickwood hedge.

Now we are in **Westgate** and on the left was Borcas Cottage as it now stands and a large garden to the end of what is now Gothic Terrace. There was a large thatched house where Galloway House stands, occupied by John Galloway, a vet. There was a cottage opposite and a small Primitive Methodist Chapel. The Minister's house was behind in Back Westgate. There was The Pillars which was a farmhouse, then the Infants' School and an old house adjoining and nothing more. I remember the trees being planted on the left hand side of the Seaton Road, before which we had a glorious view of the Mere. The Brockham stone has been there all my life and how much longer I cannot say and measured a mile from the Infants' School.

Eastgate was always beautiful but very limited. Dr. Calder's house [Ivy Lodge] was occupied then by Dr. Denton, Dr. Johns' grandfather. There was the Hall [Hornsea School,] the row of cottages adjoining Cedar Lodge; then came o farmhouse and a cottage, another one opposite and Mr. Walstead's house then no more.

There was nothing at the **Mereside** but the old white cottage still standing, the National School and the big old building on the other side which was a flourishing boarding school [bungalows] carried on by Mr. Thomas Smith, a fine stately man.

Now we come to **Newbegin**. There was a row of old houses running from Allerton's shop [Frank Hill & Son] to the Hull Savings Bank [Lloyds TSB,] four small cottages on the opposite side hiding the church, the last one abutting on the street. These were demolished and the street was widened at that point. There was a Town's pump opposite to Holly Lodge [Cusworth's] and next to Holly Lodge the Vicarage, Burn's [Hornsea Museum,] Sherwood, Bradley's. Where St. Nicholas Mount is was a high garden wall and one old whitewashed cottage at the end. Swiss Terrace was considered very stylish, Hendon Villa behind Robinson's News Shop was the last building on the opposite side. There was a farmhouse opposite the Bonnet Box [Juniper/Cariad] with a fold yard and stackyard running up to the end of Newbegin with several stacks close to the road; a high hedge, a grassy bank with a donkey grazing frequently. There was a fence and field gate across the road from what is now the Congregational Church and all beyond were ploughed fields.

There were no buildings excepting five houses in **Marine Drive**, two more further along and two old cottages which had to be taken down to save them falling down the cliff. The first **Marine Hotel** was a large building in the shape of the letter L and contained between one and two hundred bedrooms for visitors. There was a refreshment pavilion on the sands and a subterranean passage through the cliff from the hotel. This hotel was destroyed by fire; another one was built but this also was burnt down and last of all the present hotel was built.

I remember the **Parish Church** before it was restored. The pews were high backed and there was a gallery at the west end with a mahogany front. The magnificent east window was given by Lady Strickland. The Wesleyan Chapel was in Back Southgate and the Congregational Chapel is now the Mission Hall in Southgate.

Now for public life in Hornsea. There was little in the way of entertainment, perhaps an occasional concert in the National School which was always filled. In winter time we had Penny Readings and a little singing. Humorous and other readings were given by the Vicar, the Nonconformist Ministers and others. There were also occasional visits from travelling German Bands and once a dancing Russian Bear.

The coming of the railway was a real event. The first sod was turned by J.A. Wade, Esq., in a small field just where Bank Terrace is built. It was a red letter day and general holiday. A procession marched through the town to the site. A platform had been erected for the school children but when they were all on it suddenly collapsed but no one was hurt.

People lived in Hornsea and rarely went out. Before the railway was opened there were few means of travel. Stage coaches, four in hand, ran several days a week and in summer time brought loads of visitors. People used to gather in numbers at the Victoria and New Hotel

[Pike and Heron] to witness the sight. People went to Hull in carriers' carts which were without springs and it cost 1s 6d return journey. The carrier started in summer time at four o'clock in the morning and in winter at six. It took four to five hours to accomplish the journey.

Our coal supplies were brought in before the railway partly by coal vessels once or twice a year bringing about one hundred tons at once. The vessels were brought up at high tide and beached. At low tide the coal was carted away in carts with broad wheels. Mr. Martin Burn who lived in the old house [Hornsea Museum] next to the Vicarage was the agent and a few days previous to the landing went round the village soliciting orders. This supply was supplemented by carters fetching coal from Leven Canal charging 5 shillings per ton cartage. Now we pay 5 shillings per ton from the station. There was also a coal yard at Hornsea Burton, the owner being Mr. Thomas Hornsey.

We had only one weekly paper. I believe it was the Hull News, hence we got little world news.

Bathing customs were peculiar. Everyone or nearly so bathed from a machine something like a little hut on wheels. Two bathing women attended to bathe the ladies. They stepped out of the machines clad in long gowns and these women held up their heads and dipped them several times and after a good splash or two the operation was over.

I can remember three old bachelors, farmers from Rolston who were the most old fashioned men. They wore long smocks and walked with a long stick. They used to come to our shop in the Market Place but they would never come in without first knocking at the side of the door with their sticks and calling out, "Shop-keeper!" before coming in.

There were two doctors then - Dr. Denton and Dr. Harrison. Dr. Denton was a fine stately man. Blooding was commonly used for inflammatory disorders. Middle-aged people were bled in the spring instead of taking spring medicine. Children had to take treacle and brimstone. Leeches were very freely used. I have sold hundreds of leeches in my time. I myself have had four on the throat for quinsy, six on my chest for pleurisy as well as a big blister across the back for twelve hours.

A word or two about dress. Ladies wore long dresses then, with no end of flounces on them, over crinolines. A lady with a crinoline on took up all the footpath and when two ladies passed their crinolines would fly all over the place. Ladies also wore bonnets in those days which covered the head and came out in the front like a kitchen coal scuttle and tied under the chin with two pieces of ribbon. We had a straw bonnet maker in the Market Place and she made a living out of the craft. The men wore breeches and leggings and top hats - gentlemen and poor men alike - some of the top hats were very battered and green with age. One old man had a low crowned top hat. When asked how he came by it he said, "I had it given and it was over long so I took me razor, cut it in two and slopped top over bottom." In those days everybody wore night caps. Another curious custom was for men to wear smoking caps, preferably round ones fitting flat on the head and trimmed with coloured braid and a fancy tassel hanging down the left side.

There was a great deal of drinking in those days and drunkenness was very common. You might see a drunken man in the gutter swearing and howling. We had no closing hours and public houses might open all day and until much later at night. I have seen street scenes which would not be allowed today. But we had numbers of good people, godly and upright who lived in their belief.

MEMORIES OF THE PAST
by
Arthur Hobson
Born 1889

In the late 1800's Mr. Wade was the largest employer of local labour ever. Among his various interests were the Hornsea Brick and Tile Company, the building of the Hornsea-Hull Railway, farming, the first Hornsea Gas Company, his timber company in Hull and many others. The Hornsea Brick and Tile Company's buildings - now the Hornsea Potteries [Hornsea Freeport] and farming employed more than half of the working population in that time of day. My early memories of the Brickyard as we called it were its huge chimney 75 foot high; the clock on the end of the cooling sheds and the siren which sounded at 12 noon and 5:30 each day. It may be of interest to know that when the Congregational Church was built the architect, Mr. Samuel Musgrave, planned the tower to be the same height as the brickyard chimney, thus making a landmark, as he thought, for ships at sea, one at the North end and the other at the South. Architects used to plan in those days. As to the brickyard, it was a hive of industry. It had its own branch railway line leading directly to the delivery sheds, crossing where the present gates are across the allotments. The kilns for baking the bricks and tiles had a flat top covered with twelve inches of solid clay, which was always warm, and I remember having boxing matches as a boy on the top of these kilns. Mr. Wade also built what was known then as Brickyard Cottages, (now an extension of Marlborough Avenue,) which

131

were then occupied solely by workers in the yard.

The next I remember was when Mr. Wade took a partner, Mr. Cherry, the firm then being known as Wade and Cherry, the makers of the world famous Centrifugal Pumps. These pumps were exported all over the world and were shipped, not from Hull, but from Goole, the crate makers often travelling in the vans making crates for these pumps right into Goole Docks.

Mr. Wade was connected with almost every local scheme, including the first Hornsea gas works. Believe it or not but the first gas works were on the site of the present Granville Court in Cliff Road. I remember as a boy searching for sand martins' eggs in the cavity left by the removal of the gas holder. There is a fortune in gravels and sand underneath the Granville Court [housing.]

The funeral of Joseph Armytage Wade was the largest attended of any ever in Hornsea. When the head of the cortege was entering the parish church, the end was just leaving the Bridge Station. The procession, all horse drawn, (no cars in those days,) and on foot, overcrowded the church, the churchyard and into Newbegin. He was buried in the family vault on the north side of the churchyard, and the last burial in this vault was his son, Samuel Wade.

Perhaps some interest would be found in the old Hornsea lifeboat, the *Ellen and Margaret of Settle*. When the pier end was smashed by a ship my father, (who was a member of the lifeboat for over 40 years,) received the magnificent pension of £1 per year, payable on Christmas Day. However, on this occasion he walked along the pier with his hurricane lamp to see the damage. Amongst the crew of the ship were several coloured men. They were climbing from the ship up the iron structure of the pier. Dad, who had never seen a coloured man before, just dropped his lamp and ran!

In those days Hornsea had an Annual Regatta, always on August Bank Holiday, with tub races, swimming, tug-of-war, etc., and I can remember as a boy selling programmes at a halfpenny a score. Later on the whole of the pier was demolished by dynamite, which was very exciting for us youngsters. When the lifeboat was called out the bell was rung and a maroon let off, and you could hear the clap clap of the wheel covers nearly all over Hornsea.

My early recollections of old Hornsea and schooldays? I remember in the present churchyard, where the cross is now. From the main gates to the corner there were two cottages and two small shops, one of which was a watchmaker's. My father, (who always relied on Mother to get him up at 5.30 each morning and claimed he could never wake without her help), bought an alarm clock in the churchyard for two shillings and elevenpence. I have this clock today and I am eighty-four, so it must be almost a hundred years old, and still going strong. They used to make them in those days!

Schooldays I remember were at the old Infant School on Seaton Road and the Church of England School on Mereside. The first Headmaster I remember was Mr. Gilman and he was followed by Mr. & Mrs. H. Sykes. Incidently, Mrs. H. Sykes was the first "Bank Manager" in Hornsea; she ran a penny bank and a coal club along with the school. This being a Church of England School, the Vicar was the most important person and in this case it was the Reverend E.L. Tew. His favourite hymn was "Fair waved the golden corn," and as soon as he came through the school door we all had to rise and sing this hymn even though outside the snow lay inches deep! Our lot as lads was school till twelve o'clock, half an hour as errand boy; back to school till four o'clock, then more errands; taking out medicine for Dr. Johns, blowing the organ for Mr. Morrow, etc. It makes me wonder what the doctors today would say if they had all their own medicines to make, their own drugs to buy etc. There was no Health Service in those days.

Perhaps a little history about Elim Lodge may be interesting. In those days Elim Lodge was a very large estate. It covered as gardens the whole north side of Little Eastgate, all Flamborough Terrace Road, Victoria Avenue, right up to the old Marine Hotel boundary. It was then owned by Mr. T. B. Holmes and these grounds were open to the public each year on Good Friday. There was a wonderful sunken fernery with rocks and dripping water which was always interesting to us youngsters. In the grounds there was a covered tennis court for wet weather and afterwards this was loaned to the first Hornsea Gymnastic Society. I was too young to join but both my brothers were members. Mr. Thomas Barton Holmes was a very well known person and he was Chairman of the Hornsea Urban District Council for many years. The council contained many well known names including Mr. Christopher Pickering, Mr. C.E.A. Lyon, Mr. R.P. Maw and many others. In those days the council passed their own building plans and made their own bye laws. This brings me to an interesting bye law. When we built our shop premises in Cliff Road it was the only building between the Congregational Church and Elim Lodge. Our plans were passed, but with an added bye law. We were never to put on view in the window a water closet basin or anything appertaining to one. Mr. Holmes, who was a member and organist of the Wesleyan Church said he would have to pass with his wife to church each Sunday, and she would not like to see anything connected with a W.C. on view. That bye law stands today as far as I know, and was never rescinded.

Other items of interest? I remember the storm which destroyed the old promenade and the building of the first sea wall, which was from the north end of the Marine Hotel. I can remember the first orchestral concert in the open bandstand on the site of the present Floral Hall. This orchestra was led by Victor and Antonio Medcalf. Antonio was the vocal half and what a voice he had! When the wind was favourable you could hear him singing "Sons of the Sea" half way down

133

Cliff Lane.

The Council Offices were then in the old Public Rooms with two part-time officials, the Clerk and farmer Mr. Thomas Hornsey and the surveyor and architect Mr. Peter Gaskell. The roads were just dusty roads; a horse-drawn water cart sprayed them twice a day and, when anyone was very ill, straw was laid on the road to deaden the horse traffic. The first motor car I remember was owned by the Constable family at Wassand Hall. In those days I was friendly with one of the footmen employed at the Hall and he once told me that when the wind was in the right direction they could hear the old Pannod leaving Beverley and it was time to get the dinner moving.

I expect I must close this sometime so I will end with the memory of Antonio Medcalf on a still summer evening from the old open bandstand on the Prom.

> Sons of the sea, all British born,
> Sailing every ocean, laughing foes to scorn.
> They may build their ships, my lads,
> And think they know the game,
> But they can't build the boys of the Bulldog Breed
> That made Old England's name!

After 1901

My father-in-law, Mr. Johnson, owned the first motor waggonette plying between Hornsea and Bridlington. Eventually, owing to the cost of solid rubber tyres and other items, he decided to sell. He took all the family to London in it and sold it there. How did we get home? We came on a Day Excursion from King's Cross to Cleethorpes; by train to New Holland, by ferry to Hull and by train to Hornsea at a total cost in fares of just over five shillings each. The old waggonette was sold for £25 and we brought the tools home with us, as they were of more value than the old bus, and some of the tools I have today. My father-in-law always said that in the future motor traffic would take over from the railways, and how right he proved to be!

HORNSEA PRIMITIVE METHODIST
MARKET PLACE CIRCUIT
by
Walter Robinson
Born 1884

According to a history of Hornsea the Primitive Methodists built their first chapel in Westgate in 1835, the minister being the Reverend G. West, the manse being in Back Westgate and was called Clowes Cottage now called Coningsby House. It is assumed that the church was demolished and Melbourne House was rebuilt as another manse. They had two ministers at this time and it was occupied by ministers up to 1906 when one was moved to live in Swiss Terrace and the other to Wilton Terrace. I helped to move them taking out the study fittings and refixing same in Wilton Terrace.

The present Market Place church was commenced in 1864 and opened in 1865, the schoolroom being under the church at that time. The late William Robinson used to relate how, along with others, he helped to sweep it out late at night so that it could be ready for services next day. At this time Hornsea Primitive Methodist Church was a member of the Driffield Circuit along with several villages which eventually became Hornsea Market Place Circuit some time between 1857 and 1878.

On an old plan in my possession the quarterly meeting was stated to be at Driffield at 8.30 a.m., so they would have to start from home in good time. There being no buses, some of them would have to walk. (An old gentleman, a farm labourer, used to walk into Hull from Keyingham every year to be at the United Meeting which was held at King Williams Statue when I was a lad, then back again at night.)

Hornsea Camp Meeting was held on the first Sunday in July when the new minister arrived. It began at Brick Yard Cottages at the far end of Marlborough Avenue and continued with a procession stopping to sing and give short addresses at various places till noon. In the afternoon a service was held on Mere side when a waggon would serve as a platform from which short addresses were given by various speakers. At night there was a love feast in the Chapel at which biscuits and water were passed round and members gave their testimonies.

In 1895 the Trustees decided to build a new schoolroom, as the old school was overcrowded, and the opening ceremony was on October 28th 1897. In February 1902 a Trustee Meeting was held to consider lengthening the Chapel and building an alcove for the organ, adding extra pews to accommodate the congregation.

In 1905 there were the following classes:-

Sunday afternoon at 3 led by Mr. G. Usher
Tuesday night led by Miss G. Myers, G. Durn and S. Davison
Wednesday night led by T. Robinson, R. Biggins later by S. Usher and W.G. Robinson
Thursday night preaching service
Friday night class led by the junior minister
Saturday night band meeting

Christian Endeavour was commenced about this time on Mondays.

As a church, Market Place always had to work hard to meet its financial obligations but it has always been able to do it. Before Methodist union we had the Synod about once in ten years, commencing on the Friday night for the full weekend till Monday night.

There would be an open air meeting at 5.30 every Sunday night and after the service they gathered on the Chapel steps to sing. At the end of the night's service we had a prayer meeting. Seaman Davison used to kneel in the aisle to pray and G. Fletcher stood up in his pew. Certain people were very critical of some of the prayers of these people but never attempted to take part themselves. When one looks back and remembers that some of these people could neither read nor write, we have got to admit they had something that is missing today and for which we are the poorer. These people could, "Read their title to mansions in the sky," and walked by faith which showed in their lives. In conversation with some residents, one leading churchman remarked when the Market Place Chapel was mentioned, "Oh, that place, that's where all the servant girls and farm lads go." How right he was; they used to fill the gallery every Sunday night.

At one time we had an organist who shall be nameless, although he has passed on, when the minister began to preach he used to leave the chapel and visit the hostel across the way, coming back in time for the last hymn. We also had a Band of Hope and our May Queen and Festival.

August Bank Holiday was a busy day in Hornsea in those days; there was a Regatta on the beach at which sports were held with a sailing race for the fisherman's cobles as well as donkey races, pony races, foot races, tug of war, swimming races, etc. People used to come on rullys and farm waggons, and it used to be said Beverley was half empty on this day. Driffield was also well represented; the majority of the swimmers were from those two towns and used to carry off most of the prizes. One year they got a shock, We had a new minister who was a retired missionary and he had brought a native boy home with him who eventually became a minister and returned to his native land. John, as he was called, entered all the swimming races and won most of the prizes. While the rest of the swimmers were striving to get over the waves John went straight through them being used to swimming in the surf at home.

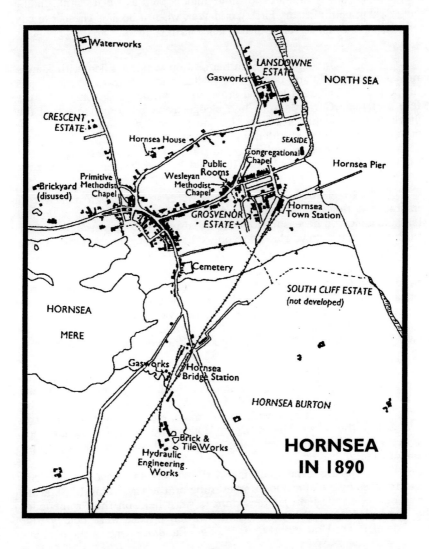

HORNSEA
IN 1890

137

REMINISCENCES OF HORNSEA
by
Mrs. E. Harry, nee Smith

N.B. Mrs Harry was the daughter of George Smith, blacksmith of Hornsea. Her father, (born 1872) and grandfather, (born 1833) had a smithy alongside 14 Market Place, (Eastgate Travel in 2002,) which was an ironmonger's shop. George Smith was a tinsmith and whitesmith, as well as a blacksmith, and he kept working until after the First World War, when it became cheaper to buy horse shoes ready made, rather than to make them.

I remember Grandfather's shop window filled with skates and customers bringing boots with skates attached to have the blades sharpened. Father used to tell a story about an ox being roasted on the Mere and Rose Carr's landau had sledge irons put on in place of the wheels to take people on a moonlit ride round Swan Island. The horse was shod with shoes studded with frost nails to prevent it slipping on the ice. When skating was over for the night the young men would sweep and flood the ice so that it would be smooth for the next days skating.

In contrast the summers were so much warmer; I can remember a huge barrel on a cart being filled at the pump on the Mereside as it was necessary to slake the dust. The cart with a sprinkler at the back would move slowly up one side of Newbegin then back down the other.

Another childhood memory was the Martinmas Hirings commencing November 23rd when the men, boys and girls came into Hornsea hoping to find work on the farms in the area. In those days a boy earned £4 a year and his keep. Stalls were set up in the Market Place as far as the Bull Ring. That week Grandfather sold tin trunks to newly hired boys and girls, giving a pocket knife or a pair of scissors to a boy or girl making a purchase.

Annual events were the Horse and Foal Show, Flower Show, Hornsea Regatta and Swimming Gala, and the Fancy Dress Carnival with decorated carts and cycles. When a circus came on to the Mereside all the performers with the animals, etc., paraded through the street before the show. August Bank Holiday was another occasion for Shipley's Roundabouts, Aunt Sally and coconut stalls to be set up on the Mereside.

During the summer the Pierrots gave open air performances in the afternoon and evening on the vacant land in Marine Drive and open air Fancy Dress dances were held on the Promenade; the band playing in the band stand. Garden parties were held in the grounds of Tower House and Cedar Lodge, Eastgate. One of the exciting moments I remember was to go to the Sunday School Treat in a waggonette, or a drive round the Mere in an open landau.

The cinema in Newbegin was called the Public Rooms until the early 1920's. [Hornsea Library] It was also the Council Offices. Concerts and dances were held in the Public Rooms before the Floral Hall was built.

Until 1924 the Waterworks on the Atwick Road supplied Hornsea with its drinking water which came from Sissons Bore Hole. The driving wheel was made from apple wood 6 to 8 ft. in diameter. We had our own pump which had never been known to run dry, even when gallons of water were needed to pour onto hot iron hoops put on to cart wheels.   My father made the railings round the Promenade when it was enclosed for the summer season; we all had season tickets then. The Park gates were all made by hand from wrought iron, every letter and scroll heated and beaten into shape. I can remember when 30 blacksmiths entered a competition in the Hornsea Horse and Foal Show. They were given a bar of iron and had to make a pair of shoes to fit a horse. After the competition all thirty of them were given tea around the kitchen table at home.

Mr. Christopher Pickering who lived at the Hall, Eastgate, [Hornsea School] built the almshouses in Newbegin. Mr. W. Sherwood's gardens in Newbegin attracted many people. He spent years making the designs in broken pot and glass.

Launching the Lifeboat was something people rushed to see after hearing a maroon fired and the bell rung from the Lifeboat Station. The carriage carrying the Lifeboat had clapper boards attached to the wheels to stop them sinking into the sand. It was drawn by 8 horses owned by local men. On reaching the sea, the horses were turned round and the boat was pushed down the launching board into the sea, the crew then used their oars and hoisted the sail. A rocket was then fired so that the ship in distress would know help was on the way.

The streets were lit by gas lamps. The lamp lighter named Partridge could be seen running from one lamp to another. When gas pipes were laid in the house it was quite an innovation. I can remember sitting at the tea table with an oil lamp in the centre and we always carried a candle upstairs. Father still sold lamps, storm lanterns and glasses for some years as it was the only lighting in some houses in Hornsea. I remember I worked in the corner shop from 8 in the morning until 7.30, to 9 p.m. on Saturdays and anytime up to midnight during Christmas week.

We grew accustomed to seeing fish carts, fruit carts, hurdygurdies with a monkey on the top, gypsies with pegs and laces in their baskets. Pot carts with the plates and dishes lying in straw, tinkers with an emery wheel to sharpen scissors and knives, all calling out their wares as they moved down the streets.

MEMORIES OF ST. BEDE'S
by
Dr. Harold ("H.I.") Loten
Born 1887

Up to 1896, Mr. Harry Elsom, F.R.G.S., was Headmaster of Holly Lodge School, now Cordock's Shop, [Cusworth's] and then built and removed to St. Bede's. I went there in its second term. In addition, he had one Master plus a French Master. Mr. H. Bishop was a very stern young man who later entered the Wesleyan Ministry and spent many years in South Africa. The French Master was Mr. Fox, who was a Frenchman, and later Mr. Studer who was a Swiss. I am not quite sure which of these two was the first. The next Master I remember was Mr. Tudor, whom we all liked. At the most there were about sixty pupils, a number of them termly boarders and a few weekly boarders. The day boys were from Hornsea and the Villages, mainly farmers' sons, Storks, Birds, Wilfords, etc.

The playing fields were on the area where College Gardens now stand - large but entirely undulating. We played football there and had a quite good cricket pitch at the top end. The only School which I can remember playing against was Eton House School, Hull. Headmaster - Mr. R.M. Pitty. P.E. was looked after by Sergeant. Hill who was in charge of the Artillery Volunteers, whose Drill Hall was in Back Southgate - now the Ex-Servicemen's Club. Sergeant Hill was one of the old brigade, strict and shouting. His expressions were like this, "Come on, smarten yourselves, you're like Chelsea Pensioners with wooden legs!" and "You're marching like a duck in a bottle."

We had no science in the School except for one morning when we were delighted to hear that we were to be taught Chemistry in the Carpentry Workshop. We went up and were introduced to bunsen burners, etc. and were delighted to be starting on this new subject. We never had another lesson and the matter was never mentioned or even hinted at again.

Mr. Elsom sold the School to Mr. W.W. Stowell, who had a board painted which said, "Principal, W.W. Stowell, B.Sc., (Inter)." We never knew what this meant. The school began to go down in numbers and was sold to Mr. Tudor who formed an Old Boys Association which did not long survive. The next were-Mr. & Mrs. Summerson who admitted girls also-after just a few years, Mr. Summerson went to join his family's engineering firm in the North. They were quite successful at St. Bede's Then came Dr. G.H. Buckmore and Rev. Hall under whose influence the School increased in standing by expanding its interest in many ways. Dr. Buckmore was a great favourite with boys and though he was not by experience an academician, he got many boys through

Scholarship examination and they obtained Bursaries in considerable numbers. Dr. Buckmore had been in the Navy in the 1914-1918 War and was a medical doctor in the Army in the 1939-1945 War. He is still living but the Reverend Hall died a year or two ago. We took the College of Preceptors exams - never the Oxford and Cambridge.

The School in the early 1900's was quite good as regards buildings. There was the "Big" room and beyond it a sizeable classroom separated by a moveable partition. When we had occasional Speech Days or School Concerts the partition was removed and the choir, etc., sat on a big platform. I remember in about 1900, one of our songs was "The Soldiers of the Queen, My Boys." This was during the Boer War. There was a carpentry workshop also - a good playground and the dining and bedroom accommodation was also quite good.

St. Bede's School, Hornsea

← St. Bede's College, Atwick Road which was attended by H.I. Loten at the turn of the 19th and 20th centuries.

SCHOOLS IN HORNSEA IN 1900
PUBLIC ELEMENTARY SCHOOLS
- Mereside (mixed) For 277 children. Master, Herbert Sykes
- Westgate Infants' For 100 children. Mistress, Miss Ganderton

PRIVATE SCHOOLS
- Miss Florence Dabb, Ladies' School, Gascoigne Villa
- Miss Kate Hall, Boys' and Girls' School, Public Rooms, Newbegin
- Leylands Boarding & Day School for Boys, Brampton House, Railway Street, Robert Reynolds, M.A., Principal
- St. Bede's College, Atwick Road, William W. Stowell, B.Sc., Principal
- Miss Mary Skinner, Southfield High School for Girls, Sandfield, Victoria Avenue
- Mrs. Annie Thom, Boys' and Girls' School, Armitage Terrace

141

BIBLIOGRAPHY

East Riding Archives, Beverley
Hornsea Parish Registers, 1654-1860
Terrier of Church Lands
Hornsea Manor Court Rolls, 1625-1769, 1769-1818
Hornsea Town Meeting Minutes Book 1849-1895
Hornsea Pier Act 1876
Hull and Hornsea Railway Act 1862

Hull Collector of Customs Letter Book 1722-1780, Customs and Excise Library, London
Copy of Domesday Book, Hull Local Studies Library
Acts of the Privy Council, 1559, 1553
A Collection of the Sufferings of the People called Quakers
Records of Admiralty Court of Oyer and Terminer
Hornsea Congregational Church Minute Book, 1818-1874
East Riding Directories for 1823, 1840, 1846, 1892
Slater's Directory 1848: Hull Directory 1858
Fretwell's Guide to Hornsea, 1893

Newspapers: Hull Packet 1787-1837; Hull Advertiser 1838-1853; Hull News 1852-1901
          Hornsea Gazette 1869-1901

Yorkshire Archaeological Society Record Series: Feet of Fines, Edward I; Wills in the York
Registry; Yorkshire Assize Rolls, Reign of John and Henry III; Yorkshire Fines;
Yorkshire Inquisitions; Royalist Composition Papers; Return of a Ninth of All Property,
Edward; Yorkshire Stuart Fines; Yorkshire Deeds; Monastic Survey; Sessions of the Peace;
Tithe Causes; East Riding Muster Rolls; Archbishop Herring's Visitation to York Diocese,
1743; Chartulary of Bridlington Priory

Bedell, E.W., An Account of Hornsea, 1848
Boyne, W., Yorkshire Tokens, 1858
Burton, E., The Georgians at Home
Du Gillon, P.H., An Abridged Version of the Hornsea Pier Negotiations, 1876
Harrison, Alan, The Rural Landscape of East Yorkshire
Heath, P., Medieval Clerical Accounts, Borthwick Institute, York, 1964
Homan, English Villagers of the 13th Century
Lambert, Malet, the Reverend, 2,000 Years of Guild Life, 1891
Lord, F., Story of Hornsea Parish Church, 1907
Lord, F., Guide to Hornsea, 1908
MacMahon, K., Roads and Turnpike Trusts in East Yorkshire
Maitland, F., Domesday Book and Beyond
Monckton, H.A., History of Ale and Beer
Nicholson, J., Beacons of East Yorkshire, 1887
Nicholson, J., Folklore of East Yorkshire, 1890
Norfolk, R.W.S., Militia, Yeomanry and Volunteer Forces of the E. Riding
Poulson, G., History of Holderness, 1841
Purvis, J., Tudor Parish Documents, Borthwick Institute, York
Round, J.H., Feudal England
Sheahan, J., History of Hull, 1864
Smith, W., the Reverend, Ancient Springs and Streams of Yorkshire, 1923

INDEX

Advertisements from 1894

145

146